SPIRITUAL
HOUSECLEANING

HEALING THE
SPACE WITHIN
BY
BEAUTIFYING
THE SPACE
AROUND YOU

KATHRYN L. ROBYN

NEW HARBINGER PUBLICATIONS, INC.

Publisher's Note

This publication is designed to provide accurate and authoritative information in regard to the subject matter covered. It is sold with the understanding that the publisher is not en gaged in rendering psychological, financial, legal, or other professional services. If expert assistance or counseling is needed, the services of a competent professional should be sought.

Distributed in the U.S.A. by Publishers Group West; in Canada by Raincoast Books; in Great Britain by Airlift Book Company, Ltd.; in South Africa by Real Books, Ltd.; in Australia by Boobook; and in New Zealand by Tandem Press.

Copyright © 2001 by Kathryn L. Robyn
New Harbinger Publications, Inc.
5674 Shattuck Avenue
Oakland, CA 94609

Yeats quote on page 4 reprinted with the permission of Scribner, a Division of Simon & Schuster, from *The Collected Poems of W. B. Yeats,* Revised Second Edition, edited by Richard J. Finneran. Copyright © 1924 by Macmillan Publishing Company, renewed 1952 by Bertha Georgie Yeats.

Charlie King lyric on page 90: "Our Life Is More Than Our Work" © 1997 Charlie King, Pied Asp Music (BMI). Reprinted with permission of Pied Asp Music.

Quote on page 42 from the Warner Bros. motion picture *Auntie Mame* ©1958 Dennis; Lawrence & Lee; Comden & Green; reprinted with permission.

Cover design by © 2001 Poulson/Gluck
Cover photograph by Michael Freeman/West Stock, Inc.
Edited by Heather Garnos

ISBN 1-57224-239-6 Paperback

All Rights Reserved

Printed in the United States of America

New Harbinger Publications' Web site address: www.newharbinger.com

03   02   01

10   9   8   7   6   5   4   3 . 2   1

First printing

For Dawn

CONTENTS

Acknowledgments

I'm lying on a raft in the pool thinking, *could life get any better?* And I'm thinking no; I have a lot to be grateful for. Besides the pool—which is the greatest of spaces—there are all these people who keep drifting into my mind's eye. These are the people who, one way or another, got me here: to the completion of this book.

First, there were all the teachers, whether contracted or inadvertent, teachers who showed me how energy works, how it moves, how to move it, and how it moves me. Healers, artists, and schoolteachers. Audience and clients, past and present participants in the healing process. There were the people whose houses I cleaned. And those whose homes I couldn't clean. There were friends, comrades on the path, and sweethearts. And there were enemies, too; antagonists who I was sure were intent on blocking me from realizing my aims, effective if complicated instructors, to be sure. I thank all these teachers as a group, many of whom are listed in the References section at the back of the book, and acknowledge each—mentor, client, friend, and foe—with honor and gratitude for the ways they have influenced my thinking and the choices I've made.

Then there were the gallant folks who helped me specifically in the production of this book. I wish to thank with the utmost gratitude my partner and my mother for reading pertinent portions of the manuscript as writers and human beings committed to genuine living, and giving their invaluable feedback—that, and for their love and friendship, which is priceless. I am also especially indebted to Sue Scheibler for her extensive notes on the manuscript and for working all the exercises—helping me to revise and getting her house clean to boot. I thank Teralis Arison for both the Zero Balancing and the truth-seeking explorations of consciousness that supported my spirit through the process; Alan Rademan for stress management methods at the end; and Beth Gramling for the magic of belief in the beginning.

My heartfelt thanks also go to the creative professionals at New Harbinger Publications, particularly Acquisitions Editor Jueli Gastwirth, Senior Editor Heather Garnos, and Art Director Amy Shoup, who have taken wonderful care of me as well as my project during the daunting process of launching the book.

Lastly, my deepest regard goes to all those women and men who have allowed me the honor of witnessing their healing and recovery in action, including those who used all or parts of this book as it was being written to supplement their program. Whether struggling with addiction, the aftermath of trauma, illness, injury, or simple ennui, they have shown me the wondrous mystery that transforms human anguish into a story of authenticity, the soul's journey toward wholeness. May this book do that route justice.

INTRODUCTION

Spring Cleaning 2001

The world is about to change. We don't know how deep or how far-reaching the change will be, even at this late date, but we can see the writing on the wall. Or rather the writing on the Web. It's the Internet that's changing everything: The way we buy. The way we sell. The way we learn. The way we teach. The way we communicate with friends, family, clients, colleagues, and governments. The way we work. It has already changed the way we play. But more important than all of this, is that the Internet is changing *where* we do all these things.

All of a sudden, we're able to shop, get a degree, and interact in effective and satisfying ways online, from home on a personal computer. This is only going to become more true and more common. Our survival, professional, and recreational needs are increasingly going to be handled over the Internet, which means that more and more people are going to be spending more and more time at home. Register your complaints about the work environment to the mirror.

As a result, we will have a chance to recreate ourselves like never before in our lifetime, or perhaps in our history. The last two millennia have been a steadily increasing whirlwind of continuous revolution of mind, body, and spirit. Culturally, most of the world has moved from an earth-centered universe with many gods, each vying for control over the fate of individuals and nations, to a noncentered universe in which each individual works to establish enough control to choose her own fate. Monarchs, once pervasive, held divine authority over thought and body alike; now the few remaining are all but figureheads in a world overflowing with democratic impulses. Disease, infection, and injury, once as immutable as geography and social standing in the power they held over experience, are now nearly irrelevant to it. The very idea of God, once matriarchal, became a patriarchal ruler to be feared and fought over, and is now developing more and more into a personal friend with whom we engage in ongoing debate as each of us struggles to find meaning in our singular lives. Those who profess to know the one true path for everyone are losing ground, as personal choice becomes the battle each nation and family must wrap its global village around. The once heretical notion that you could be whoever you wanted to be has so turned in on itself that now it's considered your own fault if you're not self-made.

Yet most of us stand at the crossroads, caught in the flux of the disputed past and the unknown future. Do we really have the opportunity to bury the dead from two thousand years of personal, political, and economic revolutions? Is it truly possible to heal the wounds from the failures of the past, and plant green fields where the blood of old exploits spilled? May we now return to our homes, declaring our selves both free and sacred? Yes we can. Just go there.

However, once home, most of us will find it not quite as we imagine freedom to be. We usually still need to clear the musty attic of our pretechnology psyches, the torturous dungeons of our pre-democratic memories, and the walled obstacles of our pre-entrepreneurial discontent. What to do with all this baggage? Don't worry. There is yet ample opportunity to put that old stuff away—to let what is behind you recede. It's time to clean house.

This book is going to take your hand and lead you through the first spring-cleaning of the Third Millennium, right in your own home. You're going to usher in a thousand years of freedom for dreams to come true, by creating a work environment that honors the soul; a play environment that secures the sacred links that make you human; a hearth to your heart; a salon to your sensibilities; a sanctuary for your mind; a bounty for your body; and a temple for your spirit. You're going to make your home a sacred space for every minute you spend in it.

CHAPTER 1

SPIRITUAL HOUSECLEANING: MAKING SACRED SPACE

Spirituality . . . is to be found and nurtured in the smallest of daily activities. . . . [T]he spirituality that feeds the soul and ultimately heals our psychological wounds may be found in those sacred objects that dress themselves in the accoutrements of the ordinary.

—Thomas Moore, *Care of the Soul*

Healing is possible. Welcome to the journey. With these simple statements, I open every support group I lead for adults recovering from substance abuse or trauma. Two hours later, I close it with another: *Healing is not only possible; healing is inevitable.* This is absolutely true. I do not add that it might take lifetimes to heal since what we are all healing from is the human condition. Clearly, healing in earnest brings about a profound patience. The beauty of working with people "in recovery" is in being witness to the kind of patience that signifies a powerful spirit to thrive. It becomes evident that healing from great challenges brings to the table precisely the skills and strategies that enrich *living with* the human condition for the long haul. It teaches us that, while the dramas of crises can spark the spirit to thrive, it is the work of a healthy life to keep the fire alight without burning down the house.

Too often though, the mundane habits of daily life tend to smother the flame inside with the cold ashes of benign neglect. We take our lives for granted. We move in and out of our homes as if they mean nothing to us, as if we mean nothing to them, as if that glorious feeling of *being alive* had nothing to do with living each day. Only now and then does something happen that causes us to comment with profound astonishment, "That got me where I live." People in recovery can be heard saying that phrase often. Perhaps that's because they know enough to search each day for a reason to live.

Sometimes it's a good feeling, sometimes it's bad, but this phrase refers to the down and dirty place within you where you completely experience yourself: your gut. Some might say it is your fundamental core, perhaps your personality, maybe the center of your emotions. Maybe it's your soul. There is no question about it when you feel something there, whether it's pain or laughter. It's where you *live*. If you lived in another time or place, another culture, you would know this place to be sacred, a place where you are most profoundly connected to everything in time and space that came together to make you who you are, the divine energy at the center of all that is. We say it is "where we live," because somewhere in the subconscious creation of language we understand that our souls expect to live in a sacred space.

It is a cliché to say, "the body is a temple," which it is not, since your body is really your whole planet; it is certainly the only place you can *be* for any extended period of time. But it is just as certainly a most sacred space, just as the planet is. What's more true, though less commonly realized, is that your home—where you actually do live—is indeed a temple. At least it should be. Your home is sacred space, a sacred space with your address. Most people think of these places as mundane. Pity. If we ever needed them to be sacred, we need it now.

Why do we need sacred space? It's simple. We need a way (a place, a process) to gently and easily reconnect with the spiritual core of being human, to be touched "where we live" on a regular basis by that divine bit of fire. When the poet W. B. Yeats wrote in his early twentieth century poem, "Things fall apart; the center cannot hold . . ." ("The Second Coming," stanza 1), he was certainly describing the dissolution more and more of us recognized as the century came to an end. Yet more also have the capacity to feel within us that divine energy linking all living things. How do we stay in touch with that feeling instead of the other? We do it by putting ourselves in a sacred space. If we're lucky, we need only go home.

A Sacred Space for Healing

So, what does it mean, sacred space? Hallowed, holy, sanctified, divine: These words can be so loaded with religious teaching they make us think of things saintly, moralistic, righteous, pious, devout. These words hold pressure to be a certain kind of "good" that scares many people away. And so they should. But when I use these terms, I'm not referring to a particular belief, dogma, or behavior within a specific group's ideology. I mean something much more innocent, more clean, more *possible*.

"Sacred" comes from a root word meaning whole. To be your own sacred self, wholly you, then, is to be connected to that divine spirit—God, Mother Earth, the Universal Life Force—however you perceive it. When you say something is sacred to you, you mean it is special to you in an intrinsic way; maybe it helps you feel more whole. Depending on where you're coming from, you may discover sacred space in a church, a temple, a mountain grove, a rocky beach, an art museum, or even the historic home of Elvis, Virginia Woolf, or Jackie Robinson.

Sacred space feels inspiring, peaceful, comforting, or healing to body, mind, or spirit. "Healing" also comes from the word for whole, of sound body and mind. When that space is your own house, it is easier to feel whole and connected in your daily life.

Walls have ears; that decor works; this room feels dead; that approach leaves room to grow; it's an open door policy; shut the door on that option; windows to your soul; glass ceiling; the lights are on but nobody's home; sweep the dirt under the rug; you made your bed, now lie in it . . .

And so on. These phrases illustrate our language's understanding of the power in your house, even if it's been buried in the attic of your subconscious. The way your house looks and functions has something to say about the way your inner being is speaking to you. In this book we will be talking about your house as an outward manifestation of your soul. In this scenario, each room represents a different aspect of you or your experience, how you take care of yourself or don't, how you incorporate others into your life or don't.

Inside your home, you keep mementos of your past that help or hinder your movement into the future. You keep the articles of warmth and refuge that help you weather the storms outside and within you. You should be able to expect this space to provide you with the means to cleanse and feed yourself, to rest your body and your mind, to engage in quality and intimate time with friends and loved ones, to entertain and stimulate you. You may take it for granted that you can unlock the door and receive these gifts of shelter every time you come home. But when you become aware of the attributes of your home that are your sacred gifts, they expand in power and importance. They lose their static condition, becoming active opportunities to heal the scrapes and scratches of a stressful day, or taking on the guardianship of tranquility when you seek refuge for healing deeper injuries. Creating sacred space in which to live enriches your whole being, mind, spirit, soul—or whatever you call the magic nothingness that makes you You. By making the space around you a sacred space, you create an environment that contributes to the healing of the space within you.

In these pages you will be asked to look at your living space as if you've never seen it before. Whatever the size and scope of it, you doubtless have a kitchen, a bathroom, a place to sleep, and a place to sit. You may do all this living in a one-room studio or in a towering estate with dozens of rooms. You may live in a tent. The size of your house is not related to the size of your soul, but the condition of your dwelling does present a picture of the condition of your being—body, mind, and spirit. Is it chaotic, spare, colorful, an afterthought? Are you a person who needs an unstructured environment, a clear routine, reminders of joy, space to feel? Does your house reflect or provide you with your needs? Could it do this better? Do you know what those needs are? Or are you ignoring that knowledge, restricting your ability to respond to the requirements of your being? Have you followed somebody else's rules and abandoned your own before you even knew what they were? You will be looking at your home's interior to see your soul's design. You will clean it, decorate it, and sweeten it in order to serve your higher being like its principal devotee.

Healing the Space

If we can speak about rooms and structures as living, organic substances, then maybe they can turn sour on us, too. If your house does not feel peaceful and exquisite, if you do not feel *at home* in it, maybe the space itself needs to be healed. To learn how to live in a healing space, spend some time learning about healing space itself. Just like anything else, concrete or ethereal, space can be torn asunder, wrenched or violated. It's easy to see when there's physical damage, of course: a cracked wall, a rotting floor, broken windows, sagging ceiling. Repairs heal physical damage. But there is more to healing space than that. There is the atmosphere behind the physical damage. Whatever happened may have left its remains lingering in the air there, like a bad smell.

Say a wall was cracked by a random act of accidental violence, such as backing into it while moving furniture. There remains a feeling of shock and remorse every time you see that damage until you can fix it. That feeling exists as the energy in the room. The energy then attaches to the furniture piece that bashed the wall. And to the reason for the moving. And to the person who was holding the furniture. Repair will clear most of the remnants, but possibly not all of it. It depends upon the power in the energy itself. For example, if the damage was caused by fire, flood, storm, or earthquake, the energy may bring more with it; the feelings attached will be more powerful if you feel more power*less*.

What's more, if the wall was busted open by a purposeful act of violence like a break-in, someone's fist, an object thrown in anger, or a drunken body lurching into it, then the feelings attached are more likely to linger even after the physical healing of repair. You may feel alienated from the space itself, and need to heal your relationship to it. You may be able to heal the attitude or temperament of the room, which is equivalent to a mental or emotional healing, by simply redecorating it—changing its appearance. Or you may need to heal the room's *spirit* by changing its energy. *Feng shui*, the Chinese art of room arrangement, is a suddenly popular and fairly effective way to do that. But if that knowledge is not available to you, there are other ways: a prayer, a party, or a ceremony, for instance. This book will show you such methods.

Many things can go wrong in a room to make it feel sick, off center, even dead. The examples above are examples of physical violation. Other external violations include insect infestations, noise, toxic odors, and construction work debris. These are all hard to come home to. Besides a cleanup, healing may be in order to create harmony with the space again.

Internal violations can trigger feelings that have the same effect, making a room feel hostile to you. You might have unresolved childhood issues that you associate with a particular room, or your fear of being alone might make a house feel dangerous to you. In addition, feelings of depression can make a house seem stifling or defeatist in its relationship to you, while perfectionism can make it seem resistant and antagonistic. When your house has these characteristics, it's not only you that needs the healing. Your house needs help, too. Sometimes the space holds energy from the previous tenant. Not just ghosts, which most people don't believe in—energy can be held in the molecules of the structure just as surely as a rug holds odors left by an untrained puppy. This book will show you ways to heal your house so that your house can heal you.

Why Cleaning?

Cleaning helps me deal with the feelings in my body.

—Louise Rafkin, *Other People's Dirt*

I know, cleaning is the last thing you want to do. Most of us will do anything to avoid it. The only time I don't avoid it is when I'm avoiding something else, like writing about cleaning. Cleaning is normally more attractive as procrastination than as a task unto itself. Like students, many writers and artists are fairly messy people, until they sit down to work. Suddenly they need to clean the floors, reorganize the cupboards, and vacuum the ceiling. The interesting thing is that once they have done all this cleaning, their heads are free and clear to face the blank page or canvas. That is because they have cleaned the debris from their creative brains and prepared their creative souls to express something unique by cleaning the space where their lives have spilled out. Perhaps the Muse likes things clean.

When I was a "starving" performance artist, I cleaned houses for money instead of waitressing like so many others did. It worked for me because I was able to be alone and rehearse or compose while doing something physically engaging. I didn't have to wear a uniform, recite the specials, or be nice. All I had to do was show up. And with the vacuum running, I could sing as loud as I wanted to.

I was taught how to clean by the first woman who hired me. She must have seen my face as I toured the rooms, daunted by the size of the job, but she didn't know she was teaching me how to see. She just gave me directions for cleaning her impossibly cluttered and overwhelmingly filthy house. I listened as she gave me a structure, a format to follow, a kind of itinerary for a pilgrim with mop and broom.

Much of it turned out to be universal: kitchen first, then dusting through the common rooms, downstairs bathroom, hallway from front door through the public part of the house, to the most private. Next, the vacuuming, and upstairs to the second bathroom, the kid's bedroom, and on to other rooms as time allowed.

An acquaintance of mine, who had also cleaned houses at one time, became unexpectedly animated when I told her about the job. She shocked me when she said, "Cleaning people's houses is just like having sex, isn't it?"

I beg your pardon?

"Everybody likes it a particular way. And each one is different."

She was right. One woman, whose kids had grown and gone, wanted all the corners scrubbed with a toothbrush. Another with teenagers still home was happy to have the cat hair vacuumed off the couch, the dirty dishes picked up off the floor, and the magazines piled neatly on the coffee table. A third, a single father, wanted the kitchen counters sparkling and bare, the stovetop scoured, and everything smelling like Lysol. Sterility was his aim.

I began to wonder: What if everyone's cleaning imperative suggested something about their inner life, reaching back in time to how those needs played out in childhood? Today, I'm sure it does. I think cleaning behaves like an indicator for how we attend or don't attend to our needs now. I will show you how every room corresponds to a part of the human body, the human mind, or the human condition. And you will learn that attending to these rooms is a way of attending to your *soul*, the name I'm going to use for that directing energy at the center of your being.

The chapters that follow will delve into each of the rooms and what they have to say to various parts of your being. For example:

- The kitchen symbolizes nurturing, the modern-day hearth around which the family gathers. Whether with food, friendship, or family, the kitchen nurtures us physically, emotionally, and communally. A sterile kitchen may indicate a starving heart.

- The bathroom, also called the washroom, restroom, and WC, supports the modern rites of purification and preparation. In ancient times you would find these accoutrements at the temple and give offerings for sacred blessing. What people feel today about their bodies' proclivities for elimination and ablution will be reflected in the ways they keep this room. Is yours a hallowed space or a profane one?

- The bedroom is for renewal. Sleeping and dreaming renew both body and mind. Reading in bed renews the self through solitude. Sex renews relationship and life force.

- The living room, parlor, den, TV, or family room—whatever it's called—maintains contact with the culture at large. But these rooms also allow for communion with the soul. They vary in design and function from formal to informal and show how we relate to both society and self. They can feel like a stateroom for visiting dignitaries or a campfire where sacred truths are told. How you keep these rooms reflects how you see yourself in terms of class, openness, and relationship to others, as well as whether you see others as friendly, powerful, or not likely to visit.

- The children's rooms will evolve as the kids grow and take increasing ownership of them until, paradoxically, they abandon them altogether. Early on, a child's room will mirror their parents' sense of themselves as guides and trainers for their child's future. But even after these rooms reverberate with the self-expression of the kids who *crash* there, they will always echo with the parents' comfort level regarding conflicting issues of creativity, dependence, and freedom. How much responsibility do you assume for your child's soul? How much do you hope to influence, manage, or regulate the soul of your child and the child of your soul?

And so on. The activity of cleaning a room or a house can be a way of finding out the meanings of these symbolic relationships. If you are paying close enough attention, it's written all over the dirt.

So, why cleaning? Four words: "Chop wood, carry water." This Zen axiom suggests that the way to inner peace is through the work of daily maintenance. It proposes that by meditating on physical essentials, the disciple will gain spiritual enlightenment, or at least liberation from the torments of the human mind. I have found the same process to occur with cleaning. But there is resistance to this extraordinary truth.

Why don't we teach, "Wipe counters, scrub floors"? Well, probably because these chores are menial, thankless, and frankly, unmanly. They do not inspire exercise or adventure; they don't provide heat or quench thirst. Wiping and scrubbing don't create; they *remove*. Comparatively speaking, chopping firewood is romantic, even glamorous; carrying water is noble, altruistic.

Cleaning, it seems, is not even respectable. Sexism and value judgments about power hold fast when it comes to cleaning. Mothers do it after the dinner has been devoured and abandoned, until they can pawn it off on their children. Maids and domestics do it while their employers are engaged in the weighty pursuits of money or learning. Dismissed as "women's work," it produces nothing, only destroying the residue of creative activity. Who wants that?

Well, I do. Because it's like healing. And if that's traditionally been women's work, then we're hoarding something special. Cleaning creates an empty space where something new—*life*—can happen, leaving a free area for a fresh approach. It creates neutral ground. More than that, this is sacred work, creating hallowed ground—a space that is returned to its cleared wholeness.

But it requires a specific kind of attention—the decidedly Zen attention of *emptiness*. Here is dirt, get rid of it. Here is garbage, take it out. Here is dust, brush it off. Wipe away the grime until the surface clears. It is valuable work. It maintains the life of a house just as healing maintains the structure of a life. With the proper attention, it leaves behind a sacred space in which to heal.

What Is Healing?

Healing is waking up to your own life. No matter what it looks like, it's yours, and it's all you've got. Healing is making a decision to care for it. You do not have to choose that—you could decide to stay asleep, to maintain the status quo. Problem is, life tends toward entropy, disorder. Things change. It's not easy to control change. But if you're awake, you don't have to control change, you can change with it.

Healing is recognizing your feelings no matter what they are. Pain, anger, frustration—these feelings are part of the human experience. They come, they go, they return. Usually, the worst has already happened. The panic that comes up today is essentially a flashback, reminding you of a previous condition of helplessness, powerlessness, hurt, or horror. If you stay with those feelings as you would stay with a troubled child, not reacting to them with panic, not judging them as either fact or fiction, they will teach you something you didn't know about what you need, or what you believe, or what you habitually do. If you are awake to those teachings, the feelings will change. So maybe the status quo wasn't so great anyway.

Healing is clearing the sacred space inside you, where you live. If you have had even minor trauma in your life—and who hasn't—there's likely to be debris in that place, a residue of feelings from incidents that separated you from that sacred place. Those ashes that, now cold and forgotten, smother the fire of your life force. If these remains were in your house, you might recognize the mess and eventually get around to cleaning it up. You might do it yourself, you might have your kids do it, you might hire someone, but you would clean it up. As it is, you just carry on, ashes piling upon ashes, threatening to put out the fire that surrounds your soul. Healing is giving that spark within you enough air to relight the fire, enough substance to keep it burning slow and steady. Healing is building a broad range of supporting resources to help you maintain the embers when the living gets too cold or too hot for you to handle on your own.

Healing has many pathways. Generally, it builds on the view that physical health, mental health, emotional stability, and spiritual well-being are connected, because healing is wholeness and wholeness is, well, *all* of you. In this way, what we call *healing* is fundamentally different from allopathic, or Western, medicine in that it aims to treat the *allness* of you—body, mind and spirit; the whole life—past, present, and future; and the whole environment—self, family, and community, rather than just the disease. Of course wholeness is elusive, so healing means being committed to the pursuit of balance and having faith in the common belief that, with the right balance of stimulation and stillness, the body heals itself; that, with love, the mind finds its own way; and that, with memories and stories, the spirit reignites, intact.

Healing is accepting your right to exist, whole or in part, as you naturally are. Not instead of or above others, but with them, along-side, in a democratic coherence. Healing is finding a democracy of the Spirit: a state of being that allows for a citizenship of the will, where you live in dialogue with God and Self, each working toward that balance of freedom and responsibility that would create an authen-tic morality—rather than under a totalitarian adherence to arbitrary codes of religious, political or social commands that locate the power of your being outside yourself in institutions. Instead, the power of your soul, its motor toward fulfillment, is located within you.

Current studies on the brain confirm that many aspects of our personality, perceptions, and perspective result from neural path-ways affected by—maybe even created by—our experiences. These pathways reside in the furrows and folds of the brain and "track" our responses to thoughts, feelings, and events. They correlate and interact with the entire body via neurotransmitters and neuro-receptors, located in organs and connective tissue, that behave like hormones, sending and receiving electrochemical messages that we perceive as feelings and sensation. When we say something like "my stomach clutched with fear," we are expressing that process in action. If that feeling of fear permeates your experience, you might say you were in a rut. Then you would be expressing the shape of your brain regarding that experience.

Healing finds ways to fill in those ruts that are too deep and narrow, encasing us in limiting patterns. It finds ways to build new pathways that broaden our capacity to fulfill our potential of joy, achievement, and intimate fellowship with others. It awakens dor-mant neuroreceptors able to pick up more pleasant messages. And it switches on neurotransmitters that have been shorted out by over- or understimulation, so that they can send a broader range of messages, again including joy.

Cleaning and healing, working on space, working on self . . . Sounds exhausting, doesn't it? Where do you get the energy? You get it from passion, that blazing spirit to thrive. Healing is locating the birth of passion. It's buried somewhere under the ashes—the aches, the cravings, the envies; in other words, it's in desire, hunger, and want. Healing is acknowledging desire even when it appears unquenchable.

Healing begins with a wish. A wish for "things" to be different, whether these things are your life, your self, or your home. Someone said, "A change is as good as a rest." Of course that's not always true. Some change stinks. (Billing statements for instance, they keep changing, they keep getting worse.) But when it is true, it's because healing is happening in that change.

Home Sweet Home

There is nothing like feeling at home in your body, feeling at home on the planet, and feeling at home in your house. When we see someone who has these characteristics, we think, "They've got it made." We associate their comfort and confidence with all kinds of unrelated qualities such as health, wealth, success, celebrity, security, family, friendship and love. It's as if we attach that "at-home" way of being to everything desirable. We see a person who doesn't need approval, and doesn't need to withhold approval. A person at the pinnacle of material and spiritual accomplishment. A self-actualized person who has found the ultimate freedom. A person we wish we were, but are not. Why aren't we this? Because we do not feel at home in our bodies or in the world. How, then, can we miss the significance of building a home that feels comfortable to be in?

Clearly, a home so sacred that you feel as accepted and acceptable in it as you would in the "bosom of Abraham," would be a boon to your own journey toward freedom, wouldn't it? A place you felt you really belonged. Still, people do not try to meet the need of *belongingness* in their homes. Instead, they keep creating (and designers keep selling) "show" homes that may be a great trophy on a shelf behind glass doors, but no place for a human being to live.

I was in a place not too long ago that had a huge spice shelf above the stove. It was really a bookshelf, but it was mounted on the kitchen wall. Very impressive. I was dazzled by the creativity of the bookshelf as well as by the gourmet potential in all those spices, and I said so. The owner dropped me right back to earth with a stop-in-the-name-of-love gesture and declared, "Oh no, those are just for show!" Not one labeled jar had ever been opened, nor would ever be. She was awed by the mess potential in creative cooking and vowed to avoid it. That was plenty of alienation for me, but she wanted me to admire her "show" living room as well. It had not one comfortable chair to sit in, and nowhere to set a cup of tea or a magazine. But a little flower cart was perched self-consciously at an angle to the door, indiscreetly exhibiting a flotilla of liquor bottles as if to exclaim, "Look how much fun we have here—we drink!" Of course very little real fun was ever had there. The casual was so studied that everyone who came through looked like cardboard cutouts. It was as if the space and all the people in it had been moved in on a WIDE LOAD truck from Stepford, wives and all.

What makes a home feel "homey," lived in, cozy, and full of life? As opposed to the trophy house where, as the saying goes, *the lights are on, but nobody's home*? Mainly, it nurtures authenticity. You can only belong somewhere that relates to you in a genuine way. If a

home is where you "hang your hat," it's a place where you are willing to drop the covering, abandon the costume, flip the lid. A dwelling becomes such when it reflects the inner being of the dwellers.
And the inner beings of these dwellers can't be a big secret to themselves or to those around them.

Then, and only then, does style come into it. When there is real
life going on in the house, that's sacred in and of itself. The potential
is always there for the sacred to rise to the level of beauty. It only
takes a little attention. But style without authenticity is a soulless
shadow. It's not a miracle; it's a mirage. Not spirit, but specter.
Marry the two—the genuine to the glorious—and even the shadows
provide solace.

There are as many ways to make your home a sacred space as
there are spaces. Whether your thing is clear and clean and Spartan,
or lush and ornate and rococo, is not the issue. To some, sacred space
implies Native American elements in a homespun Santa Fe rusticity.
To others, it's the style of the Shakers, with their philosophy of simple forms and orderly functions, that best expresses the resonance of
the Universal Spirit. You may find the modern sensibilities of the Art
Deco movement create a feeling in you of harmony between creativity and technology, allowing the sacred to work for you in an industrial world. Or you may find your inner contradictions find their
balance by an eclectic mix of classic lines and personal mementos.
The point is, the questions are what's important: "How does this or
that contribute to the wholeness of me and/or the others who live
here; how does that or this invite the healing of these shredded spirits of ours? How do we make a home sweet home for our souls in
these rooms?"

How and Why to Use This Book

So wait a minute, you're saying. "Just by cleaning my house, I can
cure myself of my body's ailments, my heart's despair, and my
mind's demons? Just by 'wiping counters and scrubbing floors,' I can
change my brain's patterns?!" Not likely, you say. And I am the first
to agree that life is terminal—we all die of it, eventually. I will even
go so far as to declare that this is not even a bad thing as far as the
entire planet goes. Dying and decaying feed the earth a balanced
diet. Not only that, but the journey from birth to death yields riches
for us humans as well. The body may be fertile in youth, but the
mind is not mature until adulthood, and the spirit comes of age only
at the time of death. But healing is happening whenever the spirit is
being tended in the living body, whenever the mind and body come

to an understanding. Healing is happening whenever your "house is in order." This book will take you through a process that helps you put and keep your house in order.

Each chapter will be roughly divided into three sections. One part will talk about the meaning of that area of the house in terms of sacred space. A second will take you through a thorough cleaning of it, healing the space. And the third will lead you through ways to let it heal you. You will be offered discussion, suggestion, digression, and exercises. The more you participate by following the exercises, working with the suggestions, thinking about how the discussion relates to your house and your life, and surrendering to the digressions, the more you'll get out of it. But that's true for anything, isn't it? Welcome to the journey home. I am thrilled to show you around.

PRACTICE PAGES

Making Space for the Sacred in YOUR House

Welcome to the first Practice Page. These pages will offer exercises in each chapter to help you turn mundane space (even if that space is only in your head) into sacred space. If you just read these pages and continue on to the next chapter, you will get something out of them, but not much. Thinking is important, yes. But if you practice them, ah! Things will begin to stir. Healing happens when thought becomes action.

Same as for cleaning. Oh, what I would give to clean my house just by thinking about it! I could throw away the latex gloves. Unfortunately, I'm afraid I would have more of a disembodied—read, sedentary—life than I already have as a writer and a healer. Also I would lose even more of the social skills in interpersonal communication than are already languishing due to the hours I spend in front of a computer. It can't be escaped; we have to do more than think to change our lives or to accomplish much of anything (even if it's just picking up the phone and calling a housecleaner to come and clean the house). These pages will propose something real for you to do, but not always cleaning. Get a pencil and a pad; we'll start with writing.

You're going to have a chance to make some lists, fill in some blanks, and begin to sketch out some clarity on at least one thing: What is sacred to you? These questions will help you figure out what is more important than anything else, at least as you have your life ordered today. Right now, look around your house to see what it's telling you about what is and is not valued.

1. Take an inventory of your house:

   a) Which room or area gives you the most pleasure?

   _____

   b) Is this your favorite room? If not, which is?

   _____

   c) Which room or area gives you the most trouble?

   _____

   d) Is this your least favorite room? If not, which is?

   _____

e) Which room or area "works" the best, that is, has the most functional organization and/or the most attractive arrangements? _____

f) Is this your favorite room? If not, why not?
_____

2. Which areas of your home "need healing?"
_____

a) What kind of attention do they need? Repair or aesthetic?
_____

b) Do they need reorganization or redecoration?
_____

3. As a child, which room was your favorite? Why?
_____

4. As a child, which room was your least favorite? Why?
_____

Charting the Cleanup

This chart will tell us what kind of situation lies ahead. No praise, no blame. Before you've read the meanings of each room, before you've gone through the process or the practice of creating space, let's see how you rate the time and trouble you're going to need to simply clean the space. At the end of the book, we'll do this again and you can compare your progress—or your *process*, if what changes is merely outlook. (Which is everything, by the way.)

1. First, calculate the time you'll spend in each room. Below are the kinds of tasks you need to do in each of six areas of your home. How long each individual job will take depends on so many subjective things that we're going to just pick an arbitrary time for most of them: five minutes per "task." Some jobs will obviously take longer than that and I've indicated those with more time in parentheses, suggesting a maximum of ten, fifteen, or twenty minutes to do. (Still, this is a wild guess, not a true estimation; it's for the rating, not for scheduling.) For each room below, there is a list of tasks that you must add up to calculate how much time cleaning yours will take. For example, if you need to do each task indicated below to clean your bedroom, your total time for that room will equal 60 minutes, which is about the longest a bedroom ever takes to clean. If, on the other hand, you only need to make the bed, your total time will be five minutes. Note these times to chart them below.

a) **Bedroom:** Shoes, hangers, hanging clothes, folding clothes, drawer organization (10), floor (15), bed, overall look and room warmth (10): TOTAL TIME = 60 minutes;

b) **Home Office:** Papers, filing (10), equipment and cords, bills (10), room efficiency: TT=35;

c) **Living Room/Den:** Dust, dirty dishes and other clutter (10), floors and rugs (15), decor, furniture (under the cushions too), cozy/comfy quotient: TT=45;

d) **Dining Room:** Table, empty space, cooking/serving accessories, room clear of extras, crumbs and sticky dregs, beauty and tranquility: TT=30;

e) **Porch:** Dirt, weeds, bugs, greenery, furniture, delightfulness: TT=30;

f) **Kitchen:** Dishes (10), counters, cabinets, stovetop, oven (30), refrigerator (15), sink, floor (15): TT=90;

g) **Bathroom:** Bathtub/shower (10), basin and accessories (10), toilet, mirrors/chrome, towels, clutter, floor/walls (10): TT=50.

2. Now you're going to chart it on the graph. On a scale of 1 to 10, the rate for using the full amount of time is a 10. So 60 minutes in the bedroom will rate you a 10, while doing just one five-minute task, such as making the bed, will rate you a 1. The values in between will be your call, estimating from 1 to 10. Draw a vertical bar on the graph below to show how you rate your rooms on that scale. This graph will give you an idea of what areas you need to concentrate on in your house, and as you progress through the book, you may want to compare this graph to what you want to concentrate on in your life.

3. Looking at your answers to the questionnaire and your chart, name *three* things you now know about yourself or your house that you didn't know before.

   a. _____

   b. _____

   c. _____

4. What, if anything, can you conclude about what is sacred and what is neglected in you or in your house?

Healing House Bar Graph

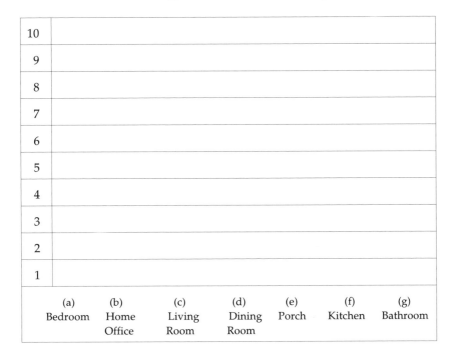

Speed Wishes

(With thanks to Julia Cameron's *The Artist's Way*, 1992)

As fast as you can, without thinking, list *ten* "speed wishes" related to your home. Wish anything. Here are some starter suggestions: Where is it? What's it look like? What does it need? What does it have? Who's in it? Who lives there with you? How does it feel to live there? Anything. **GO!**

1. _____   2. _____

3. _____   4. _____

5. _____   6. _____

7. _____   8. _____

9. _____   10. _____

CHAPTER 2

THE HEARTH:
NURTURING BODY
AND SOUL

*Everything that is used in connection with food should be
kept in a sanitary condition, and for this reason the kitchen
must be kept clean—not occasional special cleanliness, but
regular daily care of all the surfaces of the kitchen. Prevention
is always worth more than cure. . . ."*

—The Girl Scout Handbook, 1933

The first thing a sacred space provides is a world of comfort. A
space that takes good care of you in the first place prevents a
myriad of crises. How does one begin to build such a world? Do you
have the kind of friends and acquaintances that you can call on the
phone to be part of your support squad? Even if you do—and the
older you get or the more often you move, the less likely that is—it
still helps to put together your own "survival kit" for those times
when you cannot call anyone. Unfortunately, God is not the only one
who helps those who help themselves. Most people feel the same
way. So where do you start such an endeavor? You begin by making
a choice.

Imagining Nurturance

In this day and age we don't talk much about needing comfort or
sympathy or, even more maligned, *needing attention*. For many good
reasons, all having to do with learning we deserve to get our needs
met, the language has changed and now we talk about needing
support.

Choosing to get support has everything to do with making sacred space. In fact, a space does not feel remotely sacred until you feel supported in it or by it. A space that makes room for your support systems to work for you is a healing space at your service. Getting support truly is receiving the sacred in the space. But first you have to know what support is, what it feels like, what it looks like, what you feel like when you're getting it, and how to recognize when it's missing. Otherwise, how will you know when you have it? Start imagining what support looks like when you see it with your eyes, what it sounds like when you hear it, or what it feels like when it stands beside you or touches you.

Letting Your Space Support You

If you feel supported in your life, you have some indicators around you in your house. You have:

- Places available to sit and eat, read, talk, or sleep ...

- On comfortable chairs, pillows, or bedding ...

- Good lighting, bright or soft, variable by lamps, dimmer switches, or candles.

There is:

- A place for everything, you included. Ask yourself, is the space set up for you to be in and use, or is it waiting for potential visiting delegations? If it is set up for you, that's the ticket. Now, have you made room for visitors, too?

It has:

- Things that gratify your right to take up space. Do you write? If so, are there pencils around? Do you like to draw or color? Do you have a pad or book for that? Do you have allergies? If so, do you have Kleenex handy? Do you like popular culture? Or hate it? Do your TV, music, or reading environments reflect your priorities? Do you have that pet you've wanted your whole life? Have you taught him or her to live in *your* life, or are you living by someone else's rules—Mom's, Dad's, or the doggie's?

Chances are this list misses much of what you need. Take a moment and scribble in the margins what your own scenario is. Yes, write in the book: This text is just sacred enough to have room for your comments scrawled beside it. If you still can't do it, then notepaper close at hand should clearly be part of your support infrastructure.

If your home is giving you support, then it will meet a lot of your needs. When you make your home a friend in that way, you never get so desperate as to accept mere crumbs from others. You may still need a host of helpers: friends, family and professionals, a massage therapist, acupuncturist, counselor, or minister, a house-cleaner, lawn mower, laundry folder, but you'll have standards for them, as well as an understanding of your responsibility toward them, ingrained.

It is not wrong to have needs. Needing is what living beings do. You need to choose to find the amount of support you need. You may need to choose to spend the money to get it. You will also need to choose to talk to your loved ones about finding support, too, because if you're raising your standards, they are going to need help to adjust to the changes that are inevitable.

How Do You Get Support?

First you have to imagine giving it, to know it exists. Imagine giving support for someone's *bad* feelings—not a bright and cheery happy face dismissing their suffering. Here's an example from a typical parenting-education scenario:

Your five-year-old gets knocked down on the playground and runs to you for comfort, screaming hysterically. You can see that there is no visible injury. Do you:

A) Tell him to straighten up and stop being such a baby, sending him back out to play immediately?

B) Tell her if it hurts that bad, she'd better sit out the rest of playtime?

C) Pick them up, ask them where it hurts and ask them if rubbing the owie or kissing the boo-boo might help it?

The answer, of course, is (C). Unless you want your child, boy or girl, to grow up and make more toxic little people. If you love someone up, caring about the hurts, in a short while things will feel better, and regular play—or normal life—will resume. Kids who learn that "ouches" are believed, tended to, and healed grow up stronger for it.

This kind of absolute care is what many adults do not give themselves. But you can start. Give yourself attention. Get it from the way you set up your home. Where to start? Where else? In the kitchen, the place of nourishment, exemplar par excellence of nurturance.

Cleaning the Kitchen: A Recipe for Healing

Let's face it, the kitchen is the heart of the home. The heart pumps the lifeblood around the body. The kitchen organizes the support of the house. Everybody sits at the kitchen table, whether or not they are eating. If they aren't sitting, they're standing in front of the refrigerator. Maybe it's women who sit around the table and men who stand. (This would be excellent justification for men to do more of the dishes—they're already up.) Even in this era of fast food, instant gratification, and takeout, the kitchen is still the trough, the house's nurturing place where hunger and thirst are problems solved. Likewise, looking at your relationship to food and food preparation will teach you something about the way you feed your inner life.

First things first: What's in the kitchen? You've got a refrigerator full of forgotten staples and perishing perishables, dry and canned goods hiding in cupboards, cooking and serving implements lost in drawers. Dog and cat dishes are on the floor where you can regularly trip over them. You've got an overflow of cleaning items under the sink. A garbage bag, can, or compactor, if not there as well, is right nearby. But that's not all you've got. You've got your coffee maker or your teakettle all ready to go. You've got a table with a light over it. You have salt and pepper shakers. You've got napkins and place mats. You have what nurtures you in your kitchen: foods you like to eat and like to make, colors you like to look at, enough light, a comfortable place to dine, work, or visit. If your kitchen is too small for a table, you've got a pretty good facsimile of a kitchen table somewhere nearby. Whether it's a formal dining room or the coffee table in front of the TV, you know where you're taking your plate when it's time to eat. Even if you don't have these things, you fake them.

Everyone remembers the kitchen's role in their childhood. It was a room where everything that might happen did happen. Great meals and great fights. The times spent over meal preparation and making a mess were either cozy or chaotic—or both. Mealtimes were family time, and whatever the family was like was more so at the dinner table. Everyone has ideas about what to eat, how to eat it, and how much of it to eat, all wrapped up and stuffed just behind memory like leftovers crammed in the back of the fridge. Everyone knows kitchen utensils work just as well for weapons as they do for cooking. In some households, better. Boiling water, wooden spoons, butcher knives, bad cooking. Where tension, fear, or terror resided in the past, eating is guaranteed to be a problem, remembered as something to control, avoid, or minimize. On the other hand, if food was the only source of sustenance that didn't shout, hit, or molest, it might have become the cure to all inner and outer conflicts, leading to the opposite result—disordered eating.

My friend M.C., a recovering anorexic, explained her adolescent reality: "Anorexia felt like safety. It gave me a false sense of control over an inherently chaotic life." She told me about her need to take control of deprivation in a family where emotional deprivation was the rule. For many women suffering from the eating disorder *anorexia nervosa*, defined plainly as the relentless pursuit of an excessively thin ideal, dieting can turn into a refusal to take nourishment of any sort, including the emotional kind (Compton's 1995). When emotional nourishment is not available in the first place or unacceptable because of the strings attached, a complete lack of it in all forms becomes a reachable goal.

Another friend, a member of Overeaters' Anonymous, explains that food is grounding and holds the panic at bay when the energy of emotion gets too intense. For her, food is the intimate friend that gives permission to check out, asking no embarrassing questions, making no inappropriate demands. Her body and spirit feel protected by the extra layers of fat, a protection she needed as a child but didn't get from family members, who ignored the improper sexual advances of a "kindly" neighbor.

Overeaters and undereaters alike need to take care of their kitchen business. This is the room—when you neutralize it as a location, rather than a friend or a foe with its own point of view—of balanced nurturance defined on your own terms, not just balanced nutrition. It can be a place where self-care is available in abundance and in harmony with care of others. Making it that takes hands-on concentration.

First you need to remove the proverbial vermin. If your history with the kitchen leaves a bad taste in your mouth and the room gets no respect as the nurturing hub of your house, then you may have an infestation. Ants, bugs, and worms in the grain all need to be routed out. So does anger that you've stuffed, trauma that you've repressed, even a pesky relationship that's ended but not over. If these are not clarified, they will attract tics and twitches in your body and mind the same way grocery bags stashed in a corner and sticky, crumb-strewn counters attract bugs and mice.

While living in New York City, I had a visitor who was ignorant of these general principles. He had many harrowing stories of sexual abuse as a runaway teen on the streets of Los Angeles, which he eventually escaped and grew out of (as he put it), becoming highly functional in a variety of areas. But he had never fully recovered, and part of that showed up in the way he neglected our kitchen.

New York is a place where all lessons are intensified, and a week without cleaning up after himself in the kitchen, while my partner and I were away, created a nightmare takeover of thousands, maybe tens of thousands, of cockroaches. He hadn't even noticed them. Thinking of all those bugs, swarming en masse and then—after the multiple insecticide bombs—clicking dead to the floors of the cabinets, still turns my stomach. It doesn't take long for things to get out of hand. He also hadn't noticed that the love of his life was in the middle of leaving him. If you are not noticing the pestilence in your kitchen, something else in your life may be infested as well. You may use this lesson in all the places of nurturing in your life. If you want them to operate properly, you have to keep them cleaned up.

Cleaning the kitchen is a sacred practice that frees up the metaphysical sources for nurturance in your life. This activity builds or reactivates those neural pathways in your brain that track when it's time to receive proper care and balanced nourishment. Your body cannot operate without the message receptors that signal the need for nourishment, whether it's oxygen or digestible nutrients. On the flip side, they can't operate well if they don't register when the needs have been met. This is true both literally and figuratively. If you don't feel hunger, you will starve to death. If your environment is nauseating, you'll lose your appetite and starve to death in that case as well. You must be able to feel the lack in your life to know when and how to fill the hole. If your environment is not satisfying, you will stuff yourself with fluff and lies, and remain malnourished into oblivion. You will not recognize nourishment when it is staring you in the face.

Cleaning the kitchen creates an internal space for nourishment and all its equivalents to flourish—encouragement, support, desire, satisfaction and so on. When this space is kept in working order—fully stocked and clean—pests, including human ones, have no place to settle and thus stay away. Finally, like it or not, the person who takes responsibility for keeping the kitchen sacred is going to be responsible for the emotional needs of the entire household. Yet another reason to share the task.

Step 1: The Big Sweep

There are six steps to cleaning the kitchen. They are: organization, dishes, cookware, surfaces, appliances, and the floor. Don't take offense if any or all of this is old news to you; be proud of your enlightened state. Then again, if you know all this, but still do not heed it, it's time to get busy. We begin with organizing your way into the mess, preparing the space for physical nourishment. By so doing, you will create a broader range in which to nurture yourself. That means getting it organized for optimal use.

Organizing the space to create room for nurturance—whether in your kitchen or in your head—is an important part of receiving it. To begin, you need to open it up: an empty sink, an empty dish drainer, an empty shelf or counter. If there are clean dishes blocking access, put them away. If there is no place to put them away, then making an opening is the point of entry. Make it in the cupboard, on the counter, on the kitchen table, or in a bookshelf. It doesn't matter where, just make it.

While you're reorganizing, I'm wondering if you have an empty space in your life to get emotional or spiritual needs met, or is it all taken up with work and responsibilities to others? If you're not sure, the dishes will tell you. Dishes are the palettes that hold your meals. They serve up your nourishment. Maybe they also have something to say about how you accept nurturance. Take a look at them. Are they saying your nurturance comes with style or color? Natural or artistic beauty? Or are your dishes put together haphazardly, without much thought or attention. Maybe your nurturance is mixed with bitterness and regret? Dirty ones left out may stand for unfinished business with family and friends. Maybe resentment. Or, it could be a reluctance to deal with taking care of yourself, wanting— even expecting—someone else to do it for you.

How do you feel about the cooking tools of your kitchen? Can you find them, use them, and put them away without having a fit? Are they broken, rusty, chipped, and the wrong size for your needs? If there's a glitch in this system, take a look at how willing you are to go the distance to take care of yourself. On the other hand, are you a person who needs your kitchen tools to be perfect and state-of-the-art, likewise sizing up your companions on a perfectionist's scale? Or are you happy with a new one now and then to brighten the look around the history the rest hold? How does your community of friends and loved ones compare to what's in your cupboards and cabinets? How easy is this group to be with? How easy are you with them? How do you utilize the people, places, and things that feed your body, heart, and spirit? You can take small steps if change is in the air. "Healing" the room first allows the rest to change—gradually like a slow cooker.

Counters and tables (surfaces) may have to do with your superficial needs, the obvious things you need every day. For example, someone who drinks coffee every morning has her coffeemaker out. A smoothie lover never stows his blender. How do these arrangements correlate with your non-food needs—your needs for friendship or solitude, for example? Are your daily requirements spare or ample? How difficult is it to access your daily fulfillment? Do you make it easy or put obstacles in the way? Maybe you are cluttering deeper unfulfilled needs with a profusion of surface satisfactions? Or do you deprive yourself of even the simple pleasures?

My mother, who lives in a high-rise apartment with a tiny kitchen and eats out a lot, keeps her most frequently used clean dishes in the dishwasher, which she mainly employs as a drainer for hand-washed dishes. It works for her. She is not one to waste natural resources, running the dishwasher for one set of dishes, nor one to leave them hanging around, cluttering up her scene. But she likes to keep what she needs handy without going to a lot of trouble to find them. She cultivates her friendships the same way, valuing them enough to never let them stray too far nor get too complicated before she addresses the cleanup. A writer and university professor, who values both patterned artistry and plain utility, she also addressed her space problem inexpensively by positioning a tall bookshelf in her kitchen to stand for a pantry, the profusion of cans, condiments, staples, and specialty items concealed behind a festive tapestry instead of glass doors. It works beautifully.

However, her cute chairs—antique metal ice cream parlor chairs—are not at all comfortable! Because of that, or maybe for other reasons, she can often be seen leaning against her counter, plate in hand, eating standing up. Or she perches only momentarily on a chair before hopping up to go. She likes how great the little cafe set looks in front of her view of Broadway, whether it's great for lounging or not. It would be her business, not mine, to interpret the meaning of this aesthetic choice. Perhaps it is to get her out of the house where she lives alone. Perhaps long hours in the kitchen remind her of former unhappy times, so she avoids it. Maybe she just loves the historic chairs and has made the sacrifice of sentimental value over comfort. They do look fabulous at that window.

Like my mother's kitchen chairs, some of your friends may be unsettling too, but you still like them and want to keep them; so maybe you go somewhere else for a quiet sit. There are many things like this to "read" in the kitchen, and many ways to interpret their metaphorical meanings. Your kitchen is a living art installation of the ways you feed your spirit, mind, and body. It could change from day to day, or it could remain stable and predictable like an essential institution. Organize it so that it suits your personality and your needs.

If you have plenty of space, great. Luxuriate in the ease of finding what you need. Still, just like someone with lots of time and little prioritization, there's a danger of wasting your space and still not getting your needs met. Plan your space so that your glasses are together, cups together, plates stacked large to small, bowls together, etc; let your dry goods be in one area, your baking ingredients and your canned goods organized so that you don't have to rack your brain for their location every time you go to reach for them. In the same way, it will help you to organize your support system, with the addresses and telephone numbers of friends, organizations, referrals, and activities listed in places that are easy for you to find when you need them in a hurry.

If organizing your kitchen is still a task way beyond your scope, you might need assistance, which is widely available. You could check out a bookstore or library for some books and magazines on creative organizing of small or insufficient storage areas. Look into the new magazine genre started by Martha Stewart's *Living*, or the books on the market designed to help you organize your stuff, such as Julie Morgenstern's *Organizing from the Inside Out* (1998). Remember, you don't have to be as perfectly controlled as Martha is, but feel free to borrow the ideas that work. If you scan, skim, and flip through a few of these publications, you'll start generating ideas of your own. Similarly, if you haven't a clue what you need or already have in your personal resource bank, the Practice Pages at the end of this chapter will help you find out.

Now, where do you start the cleaning? That's easy: Sweep or vacuum the floor. It's easier to sweep up dust and crumbs before anything is wet. For healing purposes, this will help ground you as well. Remember, this is a holistic process. If you're allergic to dust, put on a dust mask or a bandit's bandana. Don't forget to breathe.

While you clean, empty your mind to make space for a perfect day. What would it look like, sound like, and feel like? What would you smell cooking? If any of these characteristics are in reach, you'll know at least what you want out of *this* day. If they seem remote, and feelings come up, notice them. These feelings—whether they are anger, fear, sadness, or combination feelings such as world-weariness, despair, or hopelessness—will motivate you to find out what in your life needs to change. Let tears come if they want to. Or holler over the running water. The act of cleaning becomes a working prayer to transform unmet needs into the healing power to fulfill them.

Step 2: "I Must've Been Doing the Dishes"

Some years ago, I was having coffee with a member of my extended family. Out of the blue, she asks me, "Did you know about Vietnam?" Now, my *nuclear* family has still not recovered from the screaming matches we had about that war, but it was not a topic I'd ever discussed with her. Besides, it was decades ago already. I hesitated; was there a new development I'd missed? Realizing that she meant did I know about the U.S. war in Vietnam, I answered neutrally, "Yes ma'am, yes I knew about it."

She shook her head, perplexed. "I must've been doing the dishes."

I just about spewed the coffee drip-brewed from her designer appliance. She certainly lived in another world from mine, sheltered and escapist I'd thought, but we had in common a struggle with depression. Still, I had no idea how out of touch she'd been. Should dishes require this kind of attention? No, they shouldn't. But look how well they distracted her from the unpleasantness happening to everyone around her—Vietnam was hard to miss. Maybe that was all she could do to survive.

You are welcome to use dishes that way if you must, but there are better ways. Put the radio on and tune *into* the world; let the water connect you to it. Dishes are not more important than what's happening in and around us. They are merely tools. No doubt, you could eat without them. A painter can paint from the tubes, and you could eat from the jar. But they do add a grace and congeniality to the four food groups. If yours don't, you might benefit from new dishes. The question to ask is: Do they present your nourishment in a manner that helps you savor it?

There are many standard references in slang that point to the metaphorical meanings for these implements. Have you got too much "on your plate"? Does your "cup runneth over"? What kinds of cultural activities are your "cup of tea"? Do you like to "dish" other's shortcomings with the girls? Can you take it as well as you can "dish it out"? Have you ever "cooked something up" to enliven your life? It goes on and on. Maybe women had more to do with creating the language than linguists give us credit for.

A woman in one of my support groups arrived one week with an important insight for herself and a lesson for us all. "I've just turned fifty, and for twenty-five years," she said, "I have been eating my meals on dishes that I hate. My mother gave me those dishes when I got my first apartment. They were the ones we used when I was growing up and getting criticized every night at dinner for all the ways I had not been brilliant that day. My mother gave me her old dishes and went out and bought herself a brand-new set. It was clear I was supposed to be grateful, and I accommodated her. But every meal I have eaten for twenty-five years has reminded me of how cruel she has been my entire life and how I have responded with gratitude to whatever crumb she threw my way.

"Last week after group, I don't know what happened," she continued. "I went out to buy a new quilt. I wasn't even looking at dishes. But there I was lingering in that aisle and there they were flirting back. All kinds of great dishes. I couldn't believe how much they pleased me. So I just did it. I bought a starter set." The group of about fifteen women ranging from age twenty to over fifty applauded. And she went on.

"I went home, stacked up all those old dishes of my mother's and flung them one by one into the dumpster. I heard them crash and shatter as they landed. Then I went inside and laughed through the first hilarious meal of my life. The next morning I ate an elated breakfast. All week long I served myself meals on new plates, realizing what I had been swallowing with each meal dished out on that old tainted set. Now I eat on what I know about myself. Not on her critical view of me." Everyone cheered.

Now if you have an heirloom set of china, please do not go out and trash it just because it sounds like fun. You may cherish the history in it one day. If you are already there, then you know the sacred potential in a dish as you consume your ancestry with each mouthful. If you are short on dishes, obviously you will use the same ones a lot. The same goes with friends and support people. The fewer you have, the more you call upon them. If they are precious to you, it's important to take good care of them. Be aware of tensions that fester between you, and rinse away any inedible stew with authentic but appropriate hashing out. Get the picture? Too vigorous a scrub will scratch both fine china and fine friends. For that matter, it isn't great for plastic plates or cheap acquaintances either. On the other hand, if you have people in your life who need constant cleaning up and polishing after frequent tense encounters, you may want to consider eating on paper plates. These you can just throw out after you're done with them.

Are there people who don't know how to wash dishes? Apparently there are. Follow the directions on your dishwasher's manual for stacking techniques and detergent products. I get the prize for the most dishes packed and cleaned. Experiment with the space. If you *are* the dishwasher, prerinse your dirty dishes and make sure you have a Scotch Brite brand blue sponge, backed with a white, nylon scrub pad, or its generic equivalent. It is less abrasive than the green scrub pad variety, which has a rougher countenance, and far superior in absorbency and pickup to the Brand X polyester sponges (which just push water around) and dishcloths (which don't hold the soap). With the faucet turned off, squirt a dab of liquid detergent on the wet sponge and start swabbing the wet dishes. No need to waste water filling up the sink, unless everything needs a good soak. When they're all soaped up and scrubbed clean, rinse with clear, hot running water until they squeak.

You might need special equipment to keep from scratching your supportive friends, as well. For me, it would be tape across the mouth, especially when I'm really pissed off. However, an accepting attitude and generosity of time and attention go a long way when harsh words have been spoken. Some jobs are easier with rubber or latex gloves. Some conversations go smoother with kid gloves. Harsh pads and strong words may cause scratches, but don't hesitate to use them if nothing else works. You can't go around eating out of dirty bowls and acting like everything's fine. That's how people get sick.

Step 3: Elbow Grease for Elbowroom

There are some things almost nobody likes to do. In the kitchen it's pots and pans. In the area of taking care of oneself it may be making time to be alone. Or it may be taking the time to get preventative health care, whether traditional Western or alternative. Perhaps it's getting regular exercise. They are problem chores because they take extra effort, but they are very basic to your well-being.

The best way to clean a pan is to have good quality cookware to begin with. With a little soaking, a heavy stainless steel saucepan takes the cake for even cooking and easy cleanup. Even so, soaking any pan makes it easier to wash out. Still, you may have to apply pressure and a scrubby pad to scour out the worst cooked-on remains. As for getting your family and friends to leave you alone, that may require some pressure and a no-nonsense negotiation as well. Not to mention that your own resistance to taking care of yourself may be what's cooked on.

Remember, you can't cook again until you've cleaned up the pot from the last meal. And you can't be there for anyone else unless you have the means to regroup. *What you do* during these times will be discussed in other chapters on other rooms, but *making* the time is a kitchen issue. As you scrub out the cookware from this week's dishes, think about the kind of elbow grease you will need to apply to get that kind of time. That effort will prepare your cells for elbowroom.

A Note on Special Treatments

Some pans require special treatment, just as some people and some periods in your life do. To get the best use out of the pan, treat it special. Thin-skinned nonstick pans, such as the Teflon and T-Fal brands, are coated with fragile materials that, mistreated, will scratch off, not only losing their nonstick qualities, but contaminating your food as well. All they ask is that you refrain from metal tools in their presence. But they will serve you well if you use only plastic, nylon, or nonabrasive materials to clean and cook with when using them.

Hardy cast-iron pans are stronger, but they have special needs as well. They break down into rust and all manner of deterioration if you treat them like other pans and use soaps or detergents. Bang them and scrape them with all the metal you want, but wash them with water only. Then dry them thoroughly using the heat of the burner and reseason them with a spot of vegetable oil, rubbed dry with a paper towel. If you take care of these pans in the ways they need, they will give you years of service.

Do you know what your special needs are? What makes your skin crawl? How much soaking do you require? What chips away at your emotional shields? What helps you let things go and keeps stress from sticking to you and turning to cement? Allow yourself to find out.

Congratulations, you've done all the dishes. When they're dry, put them away. Dishes are your main duty in the kitchen; ignore them at your health's peril. Doing them while angry, sad, or indifferent is time well spent, because it helps you wash away whatever foul-tasting baloney you've had to swallow during the day.

Step 4: A Clean Slate

Use a different sponge for cleaning up spills and wiping down counters than for washing the dishes. It makes sense if you think about it: The grime on the stove, dust shield, top of the refrigerator, and around the appliances is not something you want on or near anything you're going to put in your mouth. Keep your sponges and cloths fresh and clean by washing them in the laundry or a dishwasher, or by hand washing them with baking soda or a weak bleach solution. Be light on the bleach or you will rot the sponge. Letting them dry between uses or overnight keeps the mildew at bay.

Counters, of course, are not the only surfaces that need your attention. The ones that you never notice are most likely to present you with unexpected filth. Cleaning these grimy areas reminds me the most of healing. They are the Pandora's box of cleaning because every swipe of the sponge can leave a greasy smear that seems to get worse as you work on it. I'm talking about the grease, dust, and crumb grime that congregates under and behind your appliances, spices, cooking utensils, and any decorative items that might live on or near the stove, as well as on the top of the fridge, the hood over your stove, the wall behind it, and the tops and undersides of cabinets. For these areas, water is not enough. In fact, water only makes matters worse. And if you're in a hurry, you panic. This panic accounts for the exploding market for "all-purpose cleaners."

Why is it like healing? Because most of the time illness and injury sneak up on you and jump you from behind. Sure the 20/20 vision of hindsight tells you, "Ah, yes, of course it was long in coming," but the truth is that the buildup of *dis-ease* usually goes unnoticed until it spills out all over the place. Likewise, if your search for sacred space is bringing you face-to-face with unexpected pain, be patient and keep at it. Things will improve with adequate attention. If your family is panicking because your feelings are smearing their dirt around, don't be surprised. Suggest to them again that they get support of their own for being your home health *allies*. The exercises at the end of each chapter can help you contain sudden emotional turbulence to prevent your whole life from being smeared by it. Sharing these healing tasks, just like sharing cleaning tasks, can make them even more enjoyable.

In the kitchen, with or without help, strong stuff works best. Ammonia, for one. Don't sniff it for a cure; it's too toxic for most people, and besides, the cleaning metaphor doesn't go that far. But if your constitution is hearty, for *surfaces* this recipe—given me by former University of Massachusetts history professor Miriam Chrisman, a Boston Brahmin with a pilgrim's sense of independence—can't be beat. Dilute a quarter cup or less of lemon ammonia in a liter-size spray bottle of water, then add a short squirt of dish detergent. This "Yankee Cleaner" competes with the best of the store-bought brands. A nontoxic substitute I call "Dadd's Green Cleaner," (Dadd 1992) combines vinegar or lemon juice with water and a teaspoon of TSP (available at most supermarkets). It may be nontoxic, but I still wouldn't drink it.

A rule of thumb: *Rinse your sponge a lot.* For smears, use more cleaning agent and a bigger sponge. There will be dripping; some say start high and work down to clean them up, others say start low and work up to prevent them. Experiment and do what works for you. Protect your hands with gloves, your clothes from bleaching accidents, and your eyes from splattering debris. Take breaks when you need them. This job, while dirty, can be very satisfying because the results are so immediate. Your kitchen will sparkle when you've finished.

If you're ready to go, here's a ten-step method for wiping down this most nurturing room of the house. Take a chemical-free breath and remember: Healing the space leaves a sacred space in which to heal.

1. Wet the stains on the counters and stove.

2. Using your cleaner, spray the oven hood and sponge it down.

3. Rinse well.

4. Wipe the wall behind the stove in the same manner.

5. Wash spices, salt and peppers, timer, etc.—whatever rests on and around your stove area. Use the spray cleaner here, too. Make sure you don't get any of the soap or spray in the dispensers with edible foodstuffs.

6. Wipe down the stovetop and counter, including beneath and behind appliances, canisters, etc.

7. Wipe down the cabinets, doors, drawers, and drawer handles (use a toothbrush for cracks and crevices; for wooden doors, use Murphy's Oil Soap instead of dish soap), oven door, and stove knobs. Use your spray cleaner to "soak" grime; it does wonders with fingerprints.

8. Get on a sturdy stool or stepladder and tackle the top of the refrigerator. Rinse frequently. Spray a lot.

9. Save the kitchen sink for last, after you've finished cleaning for the day. Use a mild scrub sponge and a mild cleanser, bleach, or vinegar.

10. Wipe up drips or puddles on all surfaces. Polish up the chrome with a soft cotton cloth or paper towel.

Drink a glass of purifying water and behold your handiwork. You deserve to be proud. Your kitchen is starting to sparkle. I'm serious about the water: Drink a whole glass before continuing. Cold, hot, or room temperature, you choose what suits you. It will help you "rinse out" the dirt, dust, and toxic experiences that you soaked up during the work.

Step 5: Behind the Scenes

Admittedly, the focus for this chapter, and for the whole book in a way, is to help you build your larder of foods for the soul, to broaden your range of wholeness. On the side of temperance, however, I must allow for the earth-shattering point made in Barbara Graham's spoof, *Women Who Run with the Poodles* (1994). The author calls for "the right to be partial." She claims, with her tongue firmly held in cheek, that while "wholeness" is an elusive goal, "partialness" is an easy reach. I couldn't agree more. And where else but in a book on sacred space could you get written permission to be an incomplete human being, perhaps forever? Here it is, you've got it—the right to be partial. I'm partial myself.

I'm partial to fresh food, for example, cooked in simple elegance. Which brings us to the big appliances: the stove and the refrigerator. I know what you're thinking. You are exhausted, screaming inside or out loud maybe, "You mean we're not done?!" Actually, in a bona fide cleaning situation, you would do these big jobs *first* (or alone, by which I mean *only*) because they make a mess of the rest of the kitchen in the process. And they are huge jobs. Luckily they infrequently need this care.

But it's time you realized: The kitchen is an intense room. Professional cleaners will often spend nearly half a job's allotted time cleaning this one area of the house. Plus, they will contract the large appliances separately. It bears repeating: We are spending this much time on the subject of the sacred kitchen, or *what nurtures you and how to create that,* because it is the biggest issue for body and soul. Starting with this before the rest of the journey begins provides you with a foundation that will contain you when you are floundering, preventing you from foundering. If you are just too through, stop, and come back next week and do the rest of this chapter. That's okay. We're not in a race here. If you are working on the kitchen as you read and you need a break, come back and finish later. Call it a good job well done. If you've been at it all day, for God's sake quit. But if you're ready, willing and able, let's go a layer deeper.

The Refrigerator

Behind that thick closed door is where you store what goes into your body via your mouth. It holds so much promise that we open it and stare into it waiting for paradise, even when we know exactly what's in it and it's nothing. When it's full though, it's a treasure to behold, keeping fresh that which is fresh, providing quick sustenance from that which is packaged or raw. It is the be-all and end-all of metaphors for nurturance. The kid's drawings, coupons and lists, alphabet magnets, poetry-writing magnets, and paper doll magnets of Venus and David covering it only serve to show how much we love this well-lighted, atmosphere-controlled room within the room.

But it will also collect poisons and toxins if not kept clean and cold; when released, these will put you off your meal as sure as a fight at the dinner table. When it's broken, there's nothing worse than this dirty, leaking pool of a petri dish for bacteria and viruses. If there's a metaphor for acute personality disorders, then this would be it: poor thermostat control, alternately freezing and spoiling anything fresh, accompanied by noisy rumblings that threaten to shut down the motor altogether, only to rev up like normal when the repair technician arrives. The only symptom remaining during the diagnostic visit is the stench of rot permeating the monolith, which the technician blames you for keeping the door open too long.

Cleaning this two-headed ogre is one terrific way to move beyond the victimized view that "there's nothing in the world that can make me happy." Instead, when it's clean, you'll move toward, "I'm going to buy this, and I'm going to make that, and then I'll have something that'll feed me for a week!" Besides wiping down the shelves and throwing away spoiled food and other dead bodies hiding in there, cleaning the fridge means concentrating on those places where the bacteria and viruses grow.

Beneath the hydrating drawers. Often called "crispers," except by comedian Jerry Seinfeld, who calls them "rotters" because they're always full of forgotten and rotten fruit and vegetables. They're easy enough to empty out and wash with warm suds, but underneath them there is a drain where the condensation goes. When it gets clogged, it prevents proper circulation of the cooling fluids and gets gunky and gross. Put on your rubber gloves, avert your eyes, and use paper towels to get the big stuff.

In the crevices of the insulating gaskets around the doors. Don't forget to do the freezer door too. These crevices tend to turn black—that's mildew. Use a solution of baking soda or borax and water, which is easy on the rubber. A toothbrush is perfectly designed for clearing out these runners. Don't use a wet sponge in the freezer; it will stick, leaving bits of itself behind. Use a brush and a cloth instead.

In the door shelves, underneath the jars. Soak the sticky rings for a few minutes and they'll clean up faster. Oily spills will come up with your degreasing cleaning liquid of choice (my Yankee Cleaner, Dadd's Green Cleaner, or a baking soda or borax solution).

The main shelves and sides are obvious areas to clean, and not too difficult to wipe up. Again, soaking for a few minutes solves most difficulties. Sometimes a little scrubbing is necessary. Scrub lightly. No sharp implements!

Now, what do you want to put in your fancy new icebox? Start with these three things:

1. Something you really like (comfort food doesn't have to be healthy).

2. Something that's really good for you (nourishing food *does* have to be healthy).

3. Something that's very easy to grab and eat on the run (but not junk).

Now, go from there. Is there anything keeping you from making this a regular thing? If so, what could change that? Banish those bachelor shelves, empty except for two bottles: ketchup and beer. This is the symbol of how well you are taking responsibility for caring for yourself. It's your most important job. Eat up.

The Oven

In your kitchen, the oven is the essential modern hearth. It is the center of your kitchen, the only place to bake, roast, and broil in your entire house. In preindustrial times, cleaning it out would mean cleaning out the ashes and chipping away the charred debris on the sides of a huge fireplace big enough to cook and bake bread for a village feast. It was like cleaning out a modern day fireplace, only more so. It is only slightly easier with a Westinghouse.

In vernacular speech, "the oven" means the womb or uterus, as in "she's got three kids and one in the oven." Presumably, it's where new life "cooks." On a metaphysical level, that lower abdominal area of the body (for women *and* men) corresponds to the second chakra, and in energy terms relates to emotional energy, specifically emotions cooking since childhood. What remains there is all too often a storehouse of bad memories and negative energy. Cleaning out this part of your being is truly sacred work, the crux of this whole book, and essential to healing any malaise, whether mental, physical, or catastrophic. To be sure, much of humankind's search for God, soul, and self is a need to heal and fill our emotional centers, because even if there is no evidence to link an injury to a past emotion, all suffering hooks into memories of illness as a child and a yearning for the mothering that will cure it. Obviously, it is not always available.

Nonetheless, and perhaps it's no surprise, focusing on the past is something many of us want to avoid as much as cleaning out the oven. Both require a certain resolve, protective layering, and lots of helping aids, many of which only help you to throw stuff away. And while the toxic elements can be minimized, it wouldn't hurt to expect some distress.

Spills are not the horror of a dirty oven, grease is. Just as trauma is not the horror of a lousy childhood, denial is. Here is the ultimate reason to maintain a low-fat diet, or even a macrobiotic vegan one: low oven maintenance. The interpersonal equivalent to a low-fat diet? Sobriety. Living in California, I am lucky to live in a culture where nonsmoking, nondrinking, and non–drug taking friends are as common as good weather. That means I don't have a lot of pressure building up on my already hot emotional center. Possibly even luckier is the fact that I have just gotten my first self-cleaning oven and will never have to clean one again. The result, no doubt, of having healed all my emotional issues once and for all. . . . Well, we'll see.

The best alternative to avoiding it completely is this: Hire someone else to clean your oven. Pay them well. They deserve it as much as the healer you pay to clean out the sadness around your second chakra. But let's do the right thing and just clean out the oven in your kitchen.

Essential tools (*no substitutes):*

• Rubber gloves

• Loads of newspaper

• Work clothes you can ruin

• Several good sponges

• Paper towels

• Oven cleaner

I wish it were not true, but I have not found a way to clean an oven without commercial oven cleaner. I like (if I dare use such a word as "like") Easy-Off Fume Free Max, though no oven cleaner is truly tame. I have tried to do it without chemicals, yielding unimpressive results. However, unimpressive may be an acceptable balance between filthy and toxic. If it is for you, take it. Soapy water, baking soda, steel wool used judiciously, and a whole roll of paper towels can do an adequate job if there isn't much grease.

Do not use abrasives or scraping tools on your oven. It will ruin the finish that is designed to make cooking safe at high temperatures. Check your oven manual if you have one. Otherwise, assume you have an enameled or porcelain surface. (This is not the same as "baked enamel," such as is used on cookware like Le Creuset or Copco, which disallows oven cleaner.)

Optional tools (*recommended):*

• Safety glasses

• Breathing protection

If you can purchase a face mask suitable for protection from airborne chemicals, do it. Otherwise, be prepared to hold your breath. Either way, expect a chemical assault and make sure the room is well ventilated while you're using the cleaner. Keep the animals and kids out of the kitchen.

Follow the directions on the oven cleaner can to the letter. Today's "new, improved" commercial brands are available in nonaerosol and milder versions, but they are still made of lye, a dangerous substance that burns the skin and the eyes, not to mention the lungs. There are other precautions: Don't spray it on the pilot, the heating element, or light bulb (it might pop), the thermostat, or the electrical connections. This accuracy is not always easy, so *cover prohibited areas with aluminum foil.* Protect yourself from unexpected sprays, splashes, or steam reactions. In addition, it may caution against use on certain surfaces: aluminum, copper, chrome, or baked enamel. *Never use oven cleaner on continuous cleaning or self-cleaning ovens.* You'll ruin them.

Spread newspaper on the floor beneath and beyond the space occupied by the oven door when it's fully opened.

There are two methods for cleaning ovens, as indicated on your oven cleaner. For me, the best way is to spray the cleaner on a warm oven. The overnight-in-a-cold-oven method tends to be too dry for easy removal. However, the fumes are not as bad—except they're in your house all night long. Use the method that suits your needs, not mine. But this is mine:

Preheat your oven to 200 degrees Fahrenheit (just under a hundred Celsius). *Turn off the oven* and spray the cleaner evenly on the entire interior surface, avoiding the pilot, heating elements, etc. Don't forget the broiler beneath the oven if you have a gas stove. The stuff will steam and foam. Don't inhale or get it in your eyes. Close the oven door (open the kitchen door or window) and wait thirty minutes or so.

Suited in gloves and protective clothing, remove the racks and broiler pan with an oven mitt if they're still hot, and put them in the sink or bathtub, where you will clean them later. (I've read about a technique of closing them up in a plastic trash bag with ammonia or oven cleaner poured on for easier cleaning later. I haven't tried it.)

Take a good clean breath and, with your head in the oven (and the gas off!), start wiping. Nothing could put you off the oven method of committing suicide better than this job. If anything, it puts you squarely in touch with your love of fresh air. My technique is to start at the top and the rear and move forward and down toward the open door. This way, you won't be spreading fresh sludge over previously cleaned areas.

Again, rinse out your sponges a lot; use paper towels to collect any large collections of grime or debris. I have been known to sneak a scouring pad on a recalcitrant fragment or stain, but be sure to avoid scratching the oven's enameled surface and the door window glass. Rinse well, because any chemical you leave in there will cook along with your next meal, filling your kitchen with a lovely smog. Just like everything else you ever wash, the oven walls are cleaned and rinsed until they squeak. What a nasty job this is! On to the racks and broiler pans. An SOS pad is welcome now. Have at them. Take note: You may have to repeat this process if the oven's been neglected for a long time. For now though, once is plenty.

There are other methods you might try. Chapman and Major (1991) say they seldom use commercial cleaners. They recommend leaving a glass bowl of ammonia in the oven overnight and pouring salt on any spills. Heloise (1992) suggests using baking soda sprinkled on a damp sponge for not-too-grimy ovens. Debra Dadd's green method is to mix two tablespoons of liquid soap, two teaspoons borax, and warm water in a spray bottle. Whatever your method, take protective cautions for hands, eyes, and ventilation.

You will not believe the feeling of mastery that comes over you after completing this arduous task. The effort you have applied to clean out baked-on, grease-splattered food has its parallel in the effort you will have to apply to clean out baked-on patterns of getting your needs met, or not getting them met, as the case may be. These patterns have been cooking in your family for generations possibly, and greased over for as many years. But you have begun the process, and look at how you will shine. If you haven't been able to face the task of your oven, and feel only resistance to it, don't do it now. I don't care; this is not about pleasing me. But if you want to see how it makes you feel, give it a shot. You may be surprised.

When the oven is finished, clean up the newspapers and dispose of them carefully in the garbage. Wipe up drips and streaks on the outside of the oven door and on the floor. Scrub out the sink with a mild abrasive since the racks probably did a job on it.

When you're all done, step back and let yourself feel proud. If you ever had a mental job with invisible goals and no tangible results, you know how unsatisfying that can be. This experience is the opposite of that. You'll feel tired and crawly; you'll need to blow your nose and wash your face, hands, and arms. But you'll just keep staring at the inside of that oven, sparkling like a night sky in the mountains. You did that. You made those stars shine. Did it surprise you, the concentration required for so-called "mindless" work, and how fast the time passed during such "tedium"? Well, there's more.

Step 6: Grounding the Matter

The kitchen's not clean until the floor is. Here's the ideal: Sweep it daily, wipe up spots and spills as they occur. Vacuum when you do the rest of the house, and keep it mopped or scrubbed to a shine. I knew a woman once who mopped her floor twice a year and it never looked dirty. She swept it daily and wiped up spills and spots as they happened—that's it. It doesn't work that way in my house. It takes cooperation from the other tenants, including four-legged ones. This is a difficult achievement still beyond my evolution, I'm afraid. No, this leader isn't perfect, sorry to say.

If you have kids, dogs, a Julia Child way of cooking, or one of those weird uncleanable floors, you will need a scrub brush, your favorite floor clean n' shine or a non-toxic green n' clean, a big cellulose sponge or sponge mop or both, and clean water to rinse your sponge out with. The key is to never use dirty water to mop with. Always rinse out in a second bucket or even better, under the faucet, and rinse frequently.

Behold a Place to Receive

Life is a banquet and most poor sons-of-bitches are starving *to death! Live!*

—Auntie Mame

I have spent many hours on my hands and knees scrubbing other people's floors, and I found the main ingredient for deep cleaning was patience. It can be a Zen-like meditation if you let it, or a powerful prayer. I had what couldn't have been anything but a vision once while cleaning the kitchen of a woman who was in the middle of a divorce and a nervous breakdown. As palpably as a Mr. Clean commercial, the spirit of an ancient Aztec grandmother who scrubbed a stone floor and sang medicine songs appeared before me while on my hands and knees. She filled the room with light while her tears mixed with her water made sudsy with yucca root. She instructed me to envision the scrubbing out of each traumatized cell of the homeowner's body, mind, and spirit as I scoured the filthy, porous floor. She chanted in a language unknown to me as these words began to repeat in my own brain: *Clean the floor where the woman walks, cleanse the body. Clean the floor where the woman cooks, cleanse the spirit. Clean the floor where the woman eats, cleanse the heart. Wash the floor, cleanse the life. Wash the floor, begin again. . . .*

Before the image disappeared, I asked the wise woman who she was. She answered simply, "Woman Who Works." Maybe my ammonia mixture was too strong that day, or maybe I was premenstrual, but as my own tears fell into the pool of wash water, I knew how sacred this work is.

And now you know. This is how you clean the kitchen, making a space to partake of life's banquet. Not only are your outside surfaces clean, but the insides too, and the floor beneath. And all it took were time, attention, and some basic tools, protections, and protocols. Maintenance is easy once the big stuff has been handled. That's a truism.

Here also is your first taste of attempt and completion. You may not be in touch with your hunger right away. Exhaustion with the process can take desire's place for a short while. But when you do meet your hunger, your kitchen will be ready to serve you. Making the space to care for you is the hardest part of cleaning and healing. Congratulations, you're on it.

Just One More Thing

If any kitchen is going to help you feel more cared for, then it needs some genuine *hearth*like touches—essential and nonessential details that personalize it and add warmth, nourishing your other senses besides taste. Look around the room, on the table or at the walls. What is there? Focus on or acquire one thing that makes you feel welcome or cared for. For example, buy, pick, or cut yourself some flowers and place them on the table. Even a branch of green cut from a tree and propped in a jar adds some heart. Put up pictures, a drawing, or fabric that you like. Hang a string of garlic or chili peppers as embellishment, suggesting a life full of flavor and spice. Placemats, curtains, a table cloth, colorful dish towels, and pot holders all add to an ambiance that invites you to sit down and spend quality time.

I don't have a lot of knickknacks in my kitchen, but what shows gives me pleasure. Spices lined up above the stove. Canisters of tea, rice, popcorn. A bulletin board for dates, information, and coupons pertinent to the entire household. A black chalkboard clock to note things we don't want in our lives—like debt and nasty neighbors. Curtains printed with a Hopi Kachina design that seems to dance when we've done something especially wonderful.

If you are suffering with an eating disorder, or other forms of self-deprivation such as isolation, these touches are especially vital. If you have shame issues around food, you need an atmosphere that helps you heal that shame, whether you overeat or undereat. You need to affirm your right to enjoy physical nourishment, not to eat compulsively, but to shamelessly meet some needs. We all have them. How wonderful. My Kachinas are dancing.

PRACTICE PAGES

Constructing Faith to Fill Your Sacred Hunger

When my mother said grace while I was growing up, she always said the same one. It sounded like magic to me for some reason. It was the rhythm, the strange way the words were ordered, and the cornucopia it evoked in my imagination: *Bless us, O Lord, and these thy gifts, which, we are about to receive from thy bounty* . . .

Prayer is magic, of course, in that it operates on ethereal planes beyond the physical one that we can see and touch. People who believe in the power of prayer believe a Divine Will hears it and answers it with a power greater even than human imagination. They believe in Grace, Mercy, Providence. People who believe in magic believe roughly the same thing. You've done a lot of physical work in this chapter. You could do with some Grace, I think.

Your Sacred Set

Therefore, I offer you a four-part ceremony that will last you the rest of this book, or longer if you want. A ceremony is a ritualized set of actions that you set in motion to work as a prayer over time. It continues praying for you when you are doing other things. This one is to lend Grace to your table. You could also call it a Dinner Collage.

1. Purchase a place setting—at least a plate and cup. It can be as simple as a paper plate and paper cup that you decorate to please yourself, or as extravagant as a place setting of fine china and crystal that you've been eyeing for years. At least for the duration of this book, this is your Sacred Set, to satisfy your spiritual hunger. Set a special place at the table with your sacred set, or put it in another place of honor that you will encounter and notice multiple times in any day. Imbue them—either by your intention or by markers and ornamentation—with your vision of the Source of all good things. These could be anything from symbols for God or other deities, to an imaginary place where everything good in the universe is stored until dispatched to you. If you have a particular belief or faith, honor that with this spirit place setting. If you don't have one, imagine something practical like a warehouse, a mansion, a mountain cave, or lost treasure buried in the sea. Do what works for you.

2. Cut out from magazines, newspapers, photographs (or make, write, or draw) words, symbols, and pictures, graphics that represent what is missing in your life. These desires can be material, emotional, ideological, or spiritual. Anything. Everything you think would help you feel more *full-filled*. Put these bits of paper or trinkets onto your sacred plate. Arrange them like food. Continue to scout, snip, or create representations of what you want or need throughout the course of reading this book. Keep filling your plate with wishes and desires, things, people, opportunities, qualities, experiences you want to bring into your life. Invite grace by expressing your thanks every time you add to the plate. Take notice when these things begin to manifest in your life. And when they do, transfer the graphic to the cup.

3. Cut out of print media, make, write, or draw words, pictures, graphics, or other representations that express what you are grateful for having in your life already, past or present. As above, these can be people, places, or things you've experienced. Anything. Everything you understand to have enriched your life. Put these items in your sacred cup. Continue to fill your cup throughout the duration of this book. Express your thanks every time you add to this cup. Take notice when your sense of well-being begins to increase as you fill your cup.

4. Clean your kitchen. Picture your cupboards full of nourishment. Picture your table full of nurturance.

CHAPTER 3

THE DIRT YOU'VE SAVED UNDER THE LIVING ROOM RUG

> *... [A]ll the external dust and debris around you is basically a manifestation of the faults and stains within your own mind.... Therefore, as you cleanse the environment, think that you're also purifying your mind.*
>
> —His Holiness the Dalai Lama, *Path to Bliss*

I've just spent the day dusting. Not a feather dusting or a quick swipe of the TV and the side lamps, but a complete sweep of all the surfaces and everything arranged upon them—from the lamps and decor in the living room to the candlesticks in the healing room, from the photo albums on my desk to the windowsills and wainscoting. After taking all day to dust, I vacuumed the whole house in minutes. Touching every surface in the house, from the floors to the knickknacks, does something odd to you. Besides irritating the mucous membranes in your eyes and nose, it takes you inside the surface of your consciousness. Not because dusting is mindless, but because every object in your home is saturated with your spirit. In fact, when done mind*fully*, the exercises of dusting and vacuuming accomplish the creation of sacred space more completely than any other thing you can do. As you handle and tend to each and every thing, and investigate every possible step on floor and rug alike, you are pulled beneath superficial awareness into the quiet place where your soul waits for a visit.

Visiting with your soul may seem like an odd activity for the living room. It may seem like the soul would be more comfortable visiting with you in your bedroom while you dream, or in the bathtub while you soak. You would not be wrong to think these things but you would be putting limits on your soul that it doesn't have. The soul likes to visit. Period. What better room to visit in than the living room? Don't most of us do our visiting there? By all means, so does the soul.

This room in your house may be called the den, the family room, the TV room, the parlor, the front room, *downstairs*—you name it. It's the common room where you don't have to put on airs. Where you entertain guests. Where you *hang out* with family and friends, communing. Where you sit and read or watch TV or listen to music or put together a puzzle or play a game. This room is public enough to risk the interruption of your solitude, it's where you honor your need to be with people so much, you invite them over.

You may have several of these rooms and use a different one for different activities, some formal and some informal. If you do, you have the task of compartmentalizing your sacred tones. You get to be really specific, each room holding a different kind of sacred space. Take a look and see if there is one that is more soulful, and one that is decidedly less. Which one do you prefer to be in? Nonetheless, most of us have only one, and we do all our group living and much of our solitary living in it.

Hanging Out with Your Soul

The important use of the living room is, obviously, *living*. Not working, not sleeping, not washing or fixing things. It is not a doing room. It is, in fact, the only room designed for nothing else except *being*. Being and being with. Cleaning it is the practice of understanding and blessing your being-ness. That is why it produces such an opportunity for visiting with your soul, which is the part of you that does *being* best.

If the kitchen is the heart of the home, then the living room is its liver. The healing educator Rosalyn Bruyere refers to the liver as the most important organ in the body in the way it affects one's *feeling* of well-being (Bruyere 1986–1990). It can be said of the living room as well. Here you chew the fat, digesting the day. If your conversation is good, you have the opportunity to transform the events of your life into stories that add strength and sweetness to your soul. If your connections in this room are fulfilling, you can store that feeling deep within you, so that it is accessible to your ego when you need it out in the world. A good chemistry with your living room makes you feel, as Rev. Bruyere quips, more *alive-er*.

That means the living room should restore your ability to live. In this room, you interact with the vehicles of the public world (newspaper, television, radio, music, and video) in quite private ways (with no more than a handful of intimate friends or family), as a consumer rather than a producer of the media, often as background noise rather than with focused attention. If you do create here, it is most likely for the simple pleasure of energizing your soul by making music, playing games, or engaging in good conversation.

But if the chemistry is bad here, you've got bile, a jaundiced eye, cynicism about others, ineffectiveness in storing up anything from your experience that you can use for your own good, loneliness, anger, or alienation. Maybe the TV is the boss of the room like it was in the family I grew up in. Our "souls" only shared during commercials. The rest of the time all conversation sounded like, "Sh!" or "You're in the way!" or "Change the channel," which in today's technological era would sound more like, "Gimme the remote." These barked commands digest the soul itself, rather than digesting the day for the soul's benefit. You might grow up feeling cut off from your very soul.

There are many reasons for your adult soul to be cut off from your being. The psychologist and practitioner Sandra Ingerman explains in her book *Soul Retrieval* how each hit you take from birth to the present may have lopped off a part of soul and sent it flying (1991). But it doesn't have to remain so. The work of restoring your connection to it can include listening to the stories hidden in the things that inhabit your living room. You do this by the way you honor the space, especially by the way you clean it; *particularly*, the way you hold each thing to dust it. The way you get under the rugs and gather up what's been swept there. This attention is your half of the conversation with soul.

Maybe because of your early childhood experience in the living room, you don't know how to make time to be with friendly others, instead spending all your time either at work or asleep. Maybe hangout time triggers bad memories: people finding fault with your being or hurting you in an attempt to take the light of your soul for themselves. If you were violated in somebody's living room, yours today may be cluttered or barren, depending on whether you survived the abuse by cluttering your mind or by emptying it.

On the other hand, perhaps you still relate to your soul like a child. You don't bring it into the "family room," keeping it in your bedroom instead, protecting it from the judgmental eye of the public. This is a typical response of someone with stepparents, someone who may not have felt a full and welcome member of the new family when their mother or father remarried. Or maybe for some other reason—a huge family, sibling rivalry, illness, financial problems, or ideological warring among the parents—the common room where you grew up had no soul room for you in it. In these cases, where your soul's inventory should be a thick list of memories and stories, schemes and dares, you've got dust or nothing.

The conversation with your soul such as the kind dusting and vacuuming present clears the air just like a heart-to-heart talk with a close personal friend, especially if there is unfinished business between you and your own being, the so-called "faults and stains" referred to by the Dalai Lama in the chapter's opening epigraph. When you clean your living room, you take an inventory of the *stuff* in your life that holds you together—and that which holds you apart.

What kind of stuff? Everyone is dealing with some invisible emotional toxicity from the past to a greater or lesser degree, whether or not there was serious abuse. Blows to self-esteem that left no marks, transgressions that violated boundaries only indirectly, shaming remarks that caused no identifiable wounds—these are difficult to identify, and they spread like a rash, causing continual irritation. It's the dust of daily stress and strife. Sometimes it can get so thick, you can write your name in it. It covers everything. Of course you have to deal with it; you have to dust. It's not structural damage or a heavy-duty deep cleaning. It's a surface problem. Not like your being doesn't belong on the planet—more like your style can't be found at the mall. But it permeates every surface of your life and it has to be attended to regularly. These are the things you heal in your living room.

In fact, it's like taking an inventory. The stock you carry from the past, all the great stuff you've got on display or behind closed doors—literally and figuratively—came with you to this place. You may use this stuff or merely show it. Taking an inventory is finding out what all that stuff in your living room and in your self is for. If that scares the devil out of you, it's time to get that support we've been talking about, from someone who's known you a long time and remembers what you remember from long ago. Or someone new, someone who knows you only as you are today, and is not stuck on the way you were when you were thirteen, or seventeen, or twenty-eight. There have been times in my life when I needed a hundred healers to help me clear out what was beneath the surface of my anxiety. Only then did I begin the inventory that would clear out the dust that had taken the shine off my life.

I started my inventory in the middle of my training as a practitioner of natural healing. Two things happened in a matter of months to unsettle me on a deep level. First, I'd had a moped accident after which I needed a great big car around me just to get from here to there, preferably with someone else driving. That blew my style and image of myself as a self-sufficient and light-traveling free spirit. Then, I lost my job at a major record company, and with it, I believed, my dream of a songwriting career. Who was I in the world now? How would I find out?

I cleaned. I dusted my living room. And I decided to do some heavy-duty research. I wanted everything in this room purified, because I had lost the sense of my own pure being, in despair over the failure of my Great Plans. While I vacuumed, I realized that things were worse than I thought! Besides the accident and the job, I was also suffering from serious differences with my family, other disappointments in my career as a performing artist, and changes in my political affiliations as my ideologies softened. I felt that I'd been called to something, but never chosen. I was having a full-blown "identity crisis." I vacuumed beneath the couch and behind the bookcases, and dragged out all my old journals, spreading them around me. I went through them searching for evidence. I pored over the recorded feelings, dreams, and exercises that I had collected since high school. And I saw a person on a lifelong journey, a pilgrimage really, not to a specific destination, but with my very soul. Eventually, I would come to peace with that.

Taking Your Inventory

Take your time and attend to the three R's: *Record* what you feel, *report* what you learn, and *respond* to your needs as they arise. Remember you are creating more *living* room for you and your soul. You may be reacquainting yourself with parts of yourself that have been forgotten or lost in the bustle of living. Now you are making room for those parts again, if only to dust them off and see if they are still you.

Now is the time to call in helpers if you need them; this will help slow you down to a manageable pace. Find an interest group. Read or write with friends. Make weekly (daily, monthly, you choose) appointments with yourself, friends, or professional helpers to report and reflect on your *spirit's* goals. Budget your exploration like you would your finances. Sometimes these inquiries are light, easy, and "inexpensive"; they don't take a lot out of you and you can do them any time. Other times, the work on yourself is deep healing work, intensive and costly. These times need to be planned and invested in. Make a deal with yourself to only do work that puts you in an emotionally risky place when your support "team" is available. But don't use this need to plan as a way to avoid the work. Use it to pace your process so your life continues to manage itself. This is sacred time; you have permission to enjoy it. I am only advising you to not get too deep in the water without a buddy or a "lifeguard" in the vicinity.

However, do not even bother trying to push people who are emotionally unavailable into helping you. You will both only feel victimized. If someone hesitates or reacts with anger toward you rather than toward whatever happened that separated you from your deepest self, heed the warning and find someone else from whom support comes more abundantly. Don't waste precious energy fighting with others' resistance. While exploring your being, it's important to keep your discoveries as you would precious gems, displayed only when they are safe from plunder.

So how do you explore your being? Mainly, you give yourself your full attention. So, get a pen and a pad of paper, you're going to . . .

Record . . .

. . . everything you see and hear in a five minute period while sitting in your living room. Pick one of the things you see. What does it remind you of? How does it make you feel? Pick another thing. And so on. Set a timer and do it now, why don't you?

Or you could write a ten-page autobiography.

Whatever you do, read what you've recorded in past records, journals, letters, essays. Look at pictures, drawings, and tape recordings—all kinds of records. Notice how little and how fresh and innocent you were in your childhood photos. What else do you see on that face? How do you show that person whom you once were the honor she/he deserves in your house today? Make sure there's something.

Report

Sit with a friend and tell each other your life stories. Start with the first thing you remember about being in a living room. Who was there with you? What were you wearing? My first memory of the living room has to be watching *Robin Hood* on a Sunday morning with my big brother while our parents slept in. We sat about a foot away from the screen, fingers in our mouths, leaning forward on our "TV pillow horses." Then, when the commercial came on, we dragged our pillows up the stairs and "rode" those horses down. The bump, bump, bumping woke up our parents, who were recovering from a late Saturday night. It was not a wise move, but somehow we survived it. Recently I saw those same stuffed, plaid horse pillows for sale in a toy store and the whole memory came flooding back, a sweet moment from a whole other lifetime when my brother and I were allies on the range.

Respond

Some of what you find will be sweet, some sorrowful, some startling. Listen to those feelings and acknowledge them in a tangible way. Respond to them with an answer, ideally within the next forty-eight hours. A response could be a gift you buy that part of yourself, a picture you draw with your nondominant hand letting it "talk" to you, a song you play and dance to, a special meal you make to eat, a letter you write back.

Dust. An inventory is a kind of taming. Hidden places get exposed. When you are dusting and organizing, you go over everything that you keep out; when you pick something up and turn it over, you see the underside and the space left bare of dust. When I saw what I had written in my journals, the record of struggle and sometimes desperate confusion brought tears of compassion for my soul's search for herself—my soul's search for the answers that were yet to come.

In terms of cleaning house, if you don't want your things to break, you handle them gently. You keep your eyes on them. You go slowly and touch lightly. Don't rush. Don't scrub. Don't scratch. It's the same when taking your own inventory, but take even more care not to gawk. When looking this closely at portraits of your soul, use your peripheral vision, squint. Give yourself some respect. Allow your story to seep out. Try not to yank it.

"Dust, Cara."

I had a lovely woman in one of the groups I led who was a bright and talented artist. I'll call her Cara. I knew it was classic for smart and talented children to believe they should be able to manage the chaos in their families. That described Cara in her childhood. Now in her late twenties, she was managing the lives and livelihoods of several friends, all of her siblings, and her debt-addicted and demanding parents. For all of her creative brilliance, she was way too easy to exploit. Guilt was a huge tree for her, blinding her from the forest of her own life's needs.

In session after session, the group attempted to help Cara sort out her story. Why did she flinch so easily? Why all the distrust and suspicion of others? What were those feelings of grief? If she could hold so much responsibility for others, why did she feel so powerless over her own life? She was stymied; her childhood had been weird, she said, but "Nothing I couldn't handle, nothing out of the ordinary range of weird family stuff." If we were confused, you can imagine how she felt. She was in genuine pain, but she couldn't stop spinning the multitude of balancing plates long enough to see what was her experience and what was just madness.

Finally I gave her an assignment: Go home and dust, Cara. Her question to me was, "Can I just hire a cleaning lady to do it?" "Yes," I laughed. "Pay *yourself* . . . ," because so much of her struggle was tied to money, "by the hour."

The next week she didn't show up to group. The week after that I forgot to ask her and she didn't bring it up either. It was almost a month before the results were addressed. "So, Cara, did you dust?" She chuckled and nodded, "Eventually." And then she explained that she actually only started to dust last weekend. "Well, what happened?"

Cara began her story, telling us she'd put it off so long that a thick layer of dust obscured her TV screen. So she wiped it off just to see the picture. While she was at it, she dusted the CDs. Suddenly she was cleaning the lampshades and caressing the lamps, just like I'd told her to do. She polished the end tables and brushed off the upholstery, realizing that she really did love her home. She dusted things her grandmother had given her and things she'd made in art school. She said she must have been opening up to something because she went from there to the bookshelf. She had to put a kerchief over her mouth and nose, she told us, because there was so much dust. She dampened her dust cloth to keep the particles from flying around. She pulled notebooks out from behind other junk and found forgotten journals stashed away. She sat down and began to read, and then her memory opened wide. She spent five engrossed hours in page after page of ranting and raving over her parents' treatment of her, of dreams, drawings, and reports of events surrounding her family's emigration from a country enduring a revolution. Horror stories that she'd written down, forgotten, written down again and forgotten again, over a period of ten years. She closed the covers of the archives, then dusted them and the rest of the bookcase as if they were precious jewels. Not just weird family stuff.

She told us how she looked around the living room and recognized her need for living *room*. The next day, she asked her cousin, who'd been crashing in her bedroom while she slept on the couch, to move out. She told her sister she'd need to start paying half the rent. She reorganized piles of papers on her desk and purged stuff she'd been saving for other people whom she no longer saw, "just in case they would come back and need it." She filed things she still couldn't toss and paid her backlog of bills, balancing her checkbook. And each task felt to her like a prayer, she said, almost embarrassed. Like what she was doing was going *into* what she felt and thought. "Like Zen."

Then Cara laughed her own unmistakable, crystal clear laugh and said, I never got to the rest of the house, but . . . did I do it right?

Yes, I told her. Beautifully.

Begin with the Proper Tools

Don Aslett, America's self-proclaimed "#1 Cleaning Expert" and author of *The Cleaning Encyclopedia* (1993), says, "The key to dust control is using tools that *capture and remove* dust instead of just relocating it [emphasis his]. p. 123" We probably all know some people we wish we could capture and remove from our lives as well. But that's illegal, not to mention metaphysically unwise. Still, while you dust, you are welcome to visualize whisking their bad energy from your living room. Here are some suggestions for effective tools.

- Soft cotton, flannel, or terry cloth pieces (these fabrics will pick up dust and won't scratch the finish; diapers and old *cotton* towels are great).

- Specially treated cloth or paper dusting cloths (available at most supermarkets and wholesale stores).

- A feather or lamb's wool duster with a long handle. (Good for cobwebs and high or low areas, as well as when you're in a hurry and want to cheat the dusted look. Take care not to spread dust around in the air; the lamb's wool is better, but the feather is easier to use for quick jobs.)

- Vacuum cleaner with a dust brush attachment. (Great for stereo equipment, bookshelves, leather and vinyl upholstery, pictures, windows, and window coverings.) There are many new vacuum cleaners on the market that filter the dust besides sucking it up, so the finer particles don't blow back out through the mechanism. The Miele promises to filter 99.97 percent of it, down to .3 microns. Filtering vacuums are worth every extra penny; mine makes a huge difference to the allergy sufferers in my household.

- Spray, paste, or oil polish. I rarely use these because of the mess and the scent left behind, but when I do, I prefer oil polishes because they protect the wood. Twice a year is usually sufficient.

Dusting and Eliminating Clutter

There are two effective ways to dust, and you can interchange them as you work: the vacuum and the cloth. The vacuum dust brush is great because it sucks up the dust rather than spreading it around, which is a danger with cloth and a definite with feather dusters. Of course, be careful you don't suck up your small belongings. Pay attention; this is an inventory, remember?

The cloth is still going to be your principal dusting implement. Aslett's expert advice, and I agree with it, is to fold it into a nice little rectangle so you can keep turning it over onto a clean side. With a specially treated or dampened cloth, dusting is like a soothing stroke. Take time with it.

There is no denying it: Dusting and eliminating clutter are tedious jobs. Plus, your nose dries out, your eyes burn, one pile leads to another and another and another. Sometimes you live with this stuff way past your own tolerance just because you don't know what to do to get rid of it. And admittedly, it can be boring, as can taking your own inventory. You may be asking, why clean, why not just read the journals, cut to the records? Because the cleaning puts your molecules in order, prepares you to receive yourself, starts the feelings moving around. The physical labor gets you out of your rut, and things begin to happen.

When I dust I might get annoyed with the little things that I had agreed to let go of, but haven't—the unsorted clutter that belongs to someone else, the sentimental object that broke under less than stellar circumstances, the unfinished business that a certain item recalls. To *recollect* something is to let the something previously collected remind you of why you have it. The enduring feeling may or may not be pleasant, but it is a sacred moment. Stay with it long enough to allow it to register. You will have a new or deeper understanding of the message to your heart in the object. If there is no message or, worse, a hostile one, you should ask yourself why you keep something around only to collect dust. On the other hand, you might feel love for the road you've taken.

The good news is, once you know your system, you can take care of your dust problems and keep tabs on your patterns as you go along. The bad news is, it never ends once and for all. Both dust and your mind need constant attention.

Pick up the clutter first. There is nothing worse than dusting around a mess. Pick up the mislaid clothes, the crumpled wrappers, the old newspapers and magazines—everything that is not where it belongs or has served its temporary purpose. Find a correct place for it or your dusting will be fraught with frustration. That's not an inventory; it's an argument going global.

Approach clutter in an inquiring mood. Sometimes we only call those piles belonging to other people clutter. Our own stuff is an altar of talismans. Keep that in mind, allowing space for everyone's soul who lives there, and ask these things: Are these things on the shelves and tabletops things you use or appreciate, or that offer some aesthetic appeal? Or does all this stuff just protect you from knowing or feeling something about your life? Maybe you or your cohabitants are collectors, overrun with things you love, but that annoy someone else. Is there a way to accommodate both the things and the people you love by arranging these treasures in designated places such as a lovely cabinet, or the mantel, or a particular shelf? This would give them a place of honor, whereas having them everywhere and all over the place can diminish their power and uniqueness.

Try to separate the clutter of other people's stuff out of your inventory. Though it may drive you up a wall, it's possible that your spouse's or your kids' mess has little to do with your healing crisis. Before you search through the stuff as evidence for blame, consider that your current stress is not the cause, but rather the result, of habitual patterns.

On the other extreme, does your room function perfectly but offer little in the way of beauty, design, or decor? Do you have trouble displaying your beingness for other people to see? Do you then wonder why you feel alienated from them? Such a soul would benefit by a reminder of what it honors and what honors it. Maybe you could put up a picture of someone important to you, or of yourself as a child, on a table beneath a table lamp. Let something you treasure—a thing or an idea, a person or a location—have a special place out in the open. Let this artifact of your soul be seen as a reminder to you of its blessing. And as a portrait of your being that you choose to share with people whom you love enough to invite into your home.

Visiting with Soul

Your living room is the reception area of your home as sacred space. It should be decorated with things that you value and that you want the public to know you value. A vase of roses give you a vision of beauty and tells others about the part of you that appreciates such a vision. A Victorian chair speaks to you of tradition and reminds others that you value a certain protocol perhaps. And so on. You do the inquiry. Each article gives to you and expresses to others something about what you value. Make sure you do value it if you have it out. It might be whimsical, spiritual, comfortable, colorful, modern, or traditional. Whatever. Make it express your brand of sacred space.

If your living room is without comfortable seating, you have some healing to do regarding how you welcome others into your sphere. Would you really rather they didn't come? Or is it your own soul with whom you are self-conscious? Doing some of the exercises that follow will help you proceed in a good way. If your place is already cozy, warm, and *reasonably* clean, populated by things that express who you are and remind you of what you love about your life, take this in: You not only give your self a sacred space in which to hang out with your own soul, you confer healing energy on each and every person who comes to visit you by telling their souls they are accepted and acceptable. A blessing given is twice received.

PRACTICE PAGES

Tea Time for Living Room

Nostalgia and grief are common feelings to arise as you pore over the icons from your life. They can easily spill over into gossip and blame, diversions that also feel quite at home in a living room. They help to identify values that were important at one time but got lost or damaged. Here are some exercises to flush out some grief and flush away some blame, as well as to help you find some loose change that may have fallen beneath the cushions of daily life.

Why not invite some friends over to share these exercises with you?

Freewriting: Thanks to You

Freewriting is an exercise often used to give the subconscious a voice. You will need a timer to set a specific writing time. Start with a limit of five or ten minutes. Begin writing by using the prompt sentence offered below. Once you begin writing, do not stop, do not even lift your pen from the paper, do not think or edit. Just write until the timer stops you, then stop. While you are writing, if you suddenly draw a blank or don't know what to say next, just keep repeating the last word or phrase you completed, or return to the beginning sentence. This will prime the pump and in no time at all the words will start flowing again. Let them surprise you. When you are finished, try reading them aloud to your writing buddies. Visit with each other's souls.

Write for five or ten minutes, beginning with the phrase: "Thanks to you . . ."

According to Natalie Goldberg, the queen of freewriting, a subject is never covered until its opposite is addressed (Goldberg 1990). Write another beginning with "No thanks to you . . ."

Moving Meditation 1

Your emotional inventory is in your body, so you have to move to get at it. As you do this meditation in motion, bringing touch, motion, and breath to every part of your body, notice any feelings, memories, or sensations that come up for you. It will be helpful for you to read these instructions into a tape recorder, guiding the meditation in your own voice. Take care to read slowly and give yourself plenty of time to experience yourself as you go through it (Passaris 1986–89; Weaver 1984–86). Dress in comfortable, loose clothing. No shoes. Begin by sitting on the floor, but make sure you are safely distant from any objects you could run into or knock over when you begin to move around.

Close your eyes and take a deep breath. Exhale and let it all go. Inhale again, this time sending the oxygen to any place in your body that feels anxious, painful, or tense. Exhale, sending the carbon dioxide with that tension out of your mouth and to some place in the universe where it would be useful. Bring in new energy with your next inhale and fill the empty spaces in your body.

Bring your hands gently to your face, continuing this inhaling and exhaling of tension, anxiety, and pain. Massage your face softly, holding your head in your hands. Gently move your head side to side with your hands. Move it backward and forward. Exercise all the muscles in your face by opening your eyes and mouth wide and then squishing them all up like a prune. Exhale on a soft, low sound.

Keep using sound in your breath as you slide your hands down your face and neck, gently rubbing, scarcely more than a touch. Stroke your arms and torso, massaging the center of your body with the same kind attention you gave your face. Don't forget your belly and the small of your back. Pat your hips, your behind, and your pelvis. Continue to inhale deeply, humming on your exhale with a low, almost soundless note. Increase the pressure ever so slightly, pressing downward against your thighs, back and front, with the heels of your palms. Lighten up again as you softly rub your knees and the undersides of them.

Keep breathing. Notice any feelings that come up, or places where you hold your breath or tense up as you greet your body.

Knead your calves and touch your shins with the flat of your hand. Massage your ankles with your fingertips. Lean your body forward, between your knees and breathe long, sustained breaths as you stretch your back and hips with the motion. Rock back and forth, noticing your belly tighten and loosen again.

Give plenty of attention to your feet, one at a time. Rotate your ankle clockwise. Rotate in the reverse. Massage the heel, the arch, the ball, and the toes. Rub the top, too. Allow whatever sounds there are to come out. Make sound even if you don't feel it. Point your toes. Extend them back. Arch your foot, extend it back.

Slowly, when you are ready, bring yourself to standing. Put your awareness in your feet and release tension as you bring your *awareness up throughout your body, putting your full weight into the ground. Bounce on your right leg just to make sure the ground is there. Bounce on your left, finding the earth. Flex your knees, sway your hips, and swing your arms; feel the planet holding you up. Bounce on both legs, daring the world to give way. Unless your floor is unsteady, it doesn't, does it? Let your voice bounce in, too. Move in place as if you haven't a care in the world. Prepare to step out. Out loud, say **one word** that describes how you feel.*

Take a deep breath and exhale on a sound. Put your toe out in front of you and barely touch down, as if you are testing something. Look just in front of where your foot touches the ground. What do your eyes see? Say it out loud. Now, what does that remind you of? Again, say it aloud. How does it make you feel? Exhale on the word that says it.

Put your other foot out and feel lightly for the next step. What do you see or feel there, either in reality or in your imagination? Is it cold or hot? Wet or dry? What is it? Water? Cement? Coals? How comfortable would you feel stepping fully into it? Step back and repeat the test with your opposite foot. Does it feel the same or different? Stop. Look. What do you see? Say it aloud. What does it remind you of? How does it make you feel? Say it out loud. At your own pace, move into it. What are you in . . . or on? Staying in this scenario, change your pace. . . . Change your direction. . . . Change your pace again. . . . Stop. What do you see? What does it remind you of? How does it make you feel? Say it in a word.

Walk around the room. Walk fast. . . . Faster. Walk slow. Walk backwards. . . . Change your direction. . . . Change your height. . . . Walk haughty. . . . Change your pace, stay haughty. . . . Walk sneaky. . . . Change direction. . . . Change direction again. Now, walk normally. . . . Stop on a dime. What do you see? What does it remind you of? How does it make you feel? Say it out loud.

Stand quietly. Find as neutral a position as you can. Experience your body with all your senses. Notice anything, everything—memories, feelings, resistance, fun—that comes up. Notice it and let it go. Keep breathing. What do you see? Say it aloud. What does it remind you of? Aloud. How does it make you feel? Say it. Shake out your arms, your legs one at a time. Allow the planet to hold you up. Notice how it experiences you just being.

Freewriting: Now I Know ...

Record your experience of the above meditation with a freewrite beginning with "Now I know ..." And then another with "Now I don't know ..."

Finally, dust the living room. And know you are blessed.

CHAPTER 4

A Temple in
Your Bathroom

... [H]ear the soul's complaint and give it love and attention where it most needs it, even where we are most suspicious. ...

Every issue, no matter how secular it appears to be, has a sacred dimension. If you press anything far enough, you will come up against either the holy or the demonic.
—Thomas Moore, *Care of the Soul*

... Yet in my flesh shall I see God.

—Job 19:26

The Heavenly Body

Let's talk about the body. Temple or not, it's a miracle. That eyes can see and ears hear, that taste and smell and touch give you pleasure or warning, that air and water and food can keep it going for a hundred years. And that within this body a consciousness exists that is aware of itself as a separate soul. Every soul lives and breathes for its time on this one sacred planet among a universe of celestial bodies. And as such, your body merits absolute respect and care.

Unfortunately, respect for the body is the exception rather than the rule. Popular culture exalts its abuse—over and above its enjoyment—through sex, drugs, and rock 'n' roll (or other music with too much beat). Simultaneously, religious teaching maligns its very value, associating it with sin and suffering. Too many of us choose to abuse our bodies with bad care, bad food, bad thoughts, and bad medicine, addiction being the supreme deity of these. Let me be the one to say it: Your body does not deserve such disrespect, no matter how "bad" you think it is.

What's so bad about addictions if they relieve pain? We now know that an accumulation of alcohol produces disastrous results to your brain, liver, and the way your cells process nutrients. Regular use of cocaine, opiates (from heroin to Percodan), barbiturates, amphetamines, hallucinogens, and other drugs causes a melange of equally damaging disorders, destroying your brain chemistry, your muscles, and most systems of the body. Of course, so does overuse of nicotine, caffeine, and sugar. In fact, chronic excessive use of anything—which characterizes an addiction—becomes damaging to life and limb. There are plenty of so-called "acceptable" addictions besides coffee, candy, and cigarettes, from junk food to compulsive sex to unrelenting work. The abuse of addictive substances and behaviors—the kinds of lifestyles our culture exalts—allows them to interweave with your energies while providing little in return, until they tear you apart, leaving your body and soul in tatters. It is your sacred responsibility to treat yourself better than that. But the brilliant old saying, "Moderation in all things," seems harder and harder to follow with the pressures we live under today.

Struggling with an addiction is tantamount to the twelve labors of Hercules, the battle of David against Goliath, of Samson with the lion. It's a struggle of mythical, even Biblical proportions. That is because addiction is really a search for the soul concealed in the shadowed self. Truly, it is an unalleviated attempt by the heartbroken self to merge with Spirit in a culture or life devoid of it.

In pagan cultures, worshippers might alter their perception of reality with substances or ceremonies to incorporate the bodymind of the Divine. Isn't this what Christians are doing when they eat bread and drink wine at Communion to merge with the body and blood of Christ? But while contemporary believers see Christ only as the light, in the pagan view the wholeness of God is acknowledged to consist of both the light and the dark, not as opposites meeting in the middle, but as love that illuminates the unknown. By pagan, I refer to the earth-based religions of native peoples such as American Indian, European, African, and Asian shamanic traditions, pre-Christian Celtic, ancient Greek and Egyptian, etc., which divine the spirit of creation in all things, including the earth, the sky, and the underworld.

When we allocate holiness only to the light and to Heaven, casting the darkness in with the Devil, the earth, and the flesh as opposing forces of evil, we relegate much of our being to the shadows, and our very soul goes with it. We are driven to great lengths to retrieve it, to alter our perceptions so that we can see ourselves again as light and dark. Most of the time we don't even know what we're looking for. When using drugs or alcohol (a.k.a. *spirits*) today, the addict is looking to alter perception to that end, to connect with the bliss of wholeness. So is the person with bulimia, whose addiction is purgative, also a function of ancient temples and earth-based ceremonies. So too is the sex and love addict, whose addiction is the annihilation of the self, possibly in search of a vision of oneness. Oddly, a goal akin to celibate ascetics' goals.

Perhaps we are all searching, whether we know it or not, for the Divine. The trick is finding it before your addiction fills your dark places with something other than Light. It is inevitable when a body has never learned how to recognize love, and knows instead only pain or no-pain. Certainly we must be allowed to find a way to soften the unblessed harshness of real life. If you approach the care of your body as a *hallowed* act, rather than a hollow or hellish one, then you have the opportunity to alter your mind dramatically by caring for your body rather than betraying it. To do so repeatedly over time is to transform it permanently, developing a new habit out of love for life.

Of course, an addictive substance or behavior does not just alter your outlook, it also helps you escape your body, where the painful feelings or bad memories reside. When you leave your body, the psychological effect is called dissociation. It means to sever attachment to conscious awareness, usually of pain, though a lot of clarity goes along with it. Injuries, trauma, and emotional crises produce a dissociated state involuntarily, while drugs, alcohol, and ecstatic prayer create it on purpose. There are lots of reasons to want or need to escape your body and your pain, primarily bad or stressful experiences that leave you wanting to literally jump out of your skin. But *connecting* with yourself and those experiences is infinitely more caring and respectful. It's just not always so easy.

The way to start caring for your body, in showing it respect, is to learn the languages it speaks. This body knows everything about you—even things of which you are not consciously aware. And it is always trying to tell you everything it knows. But you must *listen* to it. So, where are the best acoustics in your house for listening to just about anything? Unquestionably, the bathroom.

The Bathroom: Our Postmodern Temple

Alone and naked in the bathroom, sunk in the life of the body, the life of the face, the inner life. . . . [T]ake refuge here, in the eternal now of the physical life.

—Jane Smiley, "The Bathroom"

The bathroom is your body's special temple. Not a church, mosque, synagogue, or tabernacle of any particular faith. In this temple, your body *is* the prayer. Treated with reverence, cleansed and purified of the remnants of the day or of the night, your body is prepared for rest and for power. Our daily rituals in the bathroom, once sacred rites applied by temple devotees, continue to this day, though without their sacred intentions. We bring the naked body to this place and wash it from hair to feet, just as humankind has done for millennia. We purge it of its waste and faults, flushing them away with fresh water. We shave the hair and exfoliate the skin. We scrub and shine and powder the body. We adorn it with oils, scents, fabrics and jewelry. We purge and prepare the body to our highest standards and behold its reflection before greeting and ending the day. In those times of yore the devotee would have performed these acts upon a supplicant in the temple baths as an emissary to the gods, a designated intermediary, praying for you and preparing you to receive your blessing. In today's era of spiritual democracy, individuals have the right to appeal directly to their Creator, as well as access to a bathroom, with its magnificent opportunity to do so.

Unfortunately people are more likely to associate this room with the "sins of the flesh" than with its potential for healing and enlightenment. Perhaps because of that, the bathroom, like the bedroom (with its similar associations), is an all too common setting for sexual and physical abuse. Oddly enough, the same reasons make it so suitable a temple. Your body is in its most vulnerable states while in the bathroom, whether you're bathing, sitting on the toilet, or gazing into the mirror in search of design flaws. This is the room where you confront your naked body and deal with its dirt, its waste, and its wounds. It's a fitting posture in which to seek healing and comfort, but this kind of examination is rife with frightening possibilities of horrible news under the best of circumstances. Compound that if you were molested, humiliated, punished, or compromised in any way while engaging in bathroom activities, and your body may feel, to coin a phrase, like shit.

Your body may suffer from skin problems such as abscesses, boils, infections, or rashes; digestive problems such as bowel, bladder, or kidney conditions; or cramps in muscles or uterus. Spending time in this temple can provide you with the divine energies of comfort, release, and forgiveness for your human frailties. It may be a revelation to realize that the body doesn't need extraordinary measures to be self-cleaning and self-sustaining—it was designed that way. If there's a message in your subconscious mind that your body is dirty, unchaste, or untrustworthy, and your body answers by constantly erupting in a futile attempt to purge that tainted feeling, *and* if your condition is chronic and not a specific attempt to expel some toxic element or organism, then reprogramming those messages is your task in the temple.

What happened to you may have been awful or just annoying, but that doesn't mean you are either of those things. Maybe you too have committed disturbing acts that wreak havoc on your or others' lives. You can still cleanse yourself of them and move forward. If you believe you are "cleaning out" your mind/body/soul with frequent fasting, colonics, or purgatives without professional consultation, stop now. Unless you've been eating a lot of poison, there's nothing in there to clean out! Besides, there are gentler ways to detox. Begin by cleaning your temple: the room with the basin, the tub, and the porcelain throne. Then it will cleanse you all over and all the way inside.

Tending Your Temple

Look at your bathroom in the same way you looked at your kitchen, objectively and dispassionately, sizing it up. Does it remind you of a sacred temple or a septic tank? When it's right, you will feel ready to be pampered and groomed like a holy personage. It will make you feel cozy and beautiful, handsome and sweet. If it already does, terrific. You've got the right idea. If it doesn't, then ask yourself why not.

> *Q: How do you tell a dirty bathroom?*
> *A: By the way it smells.*
>
> —Aslett (1993)

How do the smells get there? Germs, caused partly by bacteria sloughed off in the cleansing process, now breeding in a paradise of tropical humidity. And partly—let's be really frank here—by piss. Left there by some men, and increasingly by some women, who regularly miss the target and don't bother cleaning it up. What is the deal with that?

Isn't the five-gallon bowl of a toilet large enough to hit for any healthy person paying attention? If you're making this mess, stop it! Or for Pete's sake, wipe it up. This behavior is extremely disrespectful to everyone who shares the facilities with you—what *are* you thinking? It is also full of self-contempt, as all bad grooming is, whether or not that is the message you intend to convey. Would you pee on a pew? Would you mark Mecca like a dog? You would only if you were committing an act of religious contempt, which in most places would also be considered an act of war.

I know a woman who admits to contempt for other people's bodies. She is convinced they will infect her by their vicinity, so she'll wrap a toilet seat like the artist Christo wraps a building, and still she'll hover over it. Whenever I step into a stall and see a bowl so full of paper it's soaked up all the water, I suspect she's been there. This behavior is very resistant to change. No amount of medical research showing the extreme difficulty of contracting any disease (except maybe a pulled hamstring) from a toilet seat can persuade her to sit on the darn thing. I wouldn't clean a bathroom she's been in. She insists she never misses, but I won't take the chance. This brings up the most important piece of equipment for cleaning bathrooms:

- A good pair of rubber or latex gloves.

There are differing opinions as to keeping a clean bathroom. Aslett, and apparently many institutional and industrial practitioners, believe in the prolific use of the disinfectant spray cleaner. He insists five minutes a day armed with a product like Lysol in a spray bottle and a white nylon-backed scrub sponge will keep your bathroom "fresh-smelling and clean all the time." It's not for me. My bet is that many of these guys are just spraying the foul-smelling stuff around because people associate that smell with sterile conditions. But disinfectants can be irritating to your membranes, if not toxic to your system. Anything that smells like a hosed-down stairwell in a parking garage is not my idea of a pristine temple. *Clean can smell sweet.*

As a dirty kitchen makes for a dirty house, then a filthy bathroom fouls your whole body. If bacteria like strep and staph are in paradise here, your health is at risk. When someone hates their body, it will show up in either a disgusting or an antiseptic bathroom. If you are used to such conditions to the extent you don't notice them, then your life will change forever once you learn to clean it up properly. Not just the way our twentieth-century understanding of sanitation changed the world, ushering in a modern era of greater health and longer life spans, though you shouldn't miss out on that. And not just the way relaxing a bit about sterility makes the difference between a home where people live and a hospital where they die. But because getting used to caring for your body in conditions that are clean, lush, and lovely will elevate your sense of worth and worthiness.

It's true, cleaning the john is a dirty job, but somebody's got to do it. If it's your bathroom, then it needs to be you. Take notice of what grosses you out in your own bathroom and use that information to start transforming your *shithouse* or your disinfecting chamber into a temple bathhouse. In ancient Egyptian and Greek temples, the lowly job of cleaning the ceremonial baths was the highest assignment of sacred service. Approach your bathroom with that kind of reverence.

Here's what you do:

1. Sweep or vacuum the floor first. Hair, which is the bathroom floor's favorite covering, is much easier to pick up when dry. I am in love with my Dustbuster for this frequent job.

2. Wet your sponge, splashing the tub and sink with warm water.

3. Sprinkle or spray the cleaning product of your choice in the toilet bowl, around the tub and shower walls and fixtures, as well as in the sink.

4. Dust shelves, ledges, windowsills, etc. using a dampened cotton cloth or towel. Wipe the bottles and jars, tubes and appliances. Perfumes, powders, lotions and sprays. Jewelry, razors, brush, and comb. Magazines, soaps, blow dryer. Mirrors. Dust them with a dry or damp cloth, wipe away fingerprints or sticky residue of soaps, gels, etc. Let them dry off before you put them back.

5. Attend to the insides *and* outsides of the toilet, tub, and shower, with sanitation the predominant theme. This is the hands-and-knees kind of a job that can leave you feeling pretty lowly. Every story of a great spiritual teacher depicts them, at some point, humbling themselves on their knees in sacrifice, serving their followers. This is to show the ultimate worthiness of menial tasks, even the lowliest. And you can't get much lowlier than cleaning out a toilet. Humility, not humiliation, serves us all. Complete this task, not in shame, but in service to all your body's needs and functions. If you are cleaning someone else's mess, that does not make you inferior to them. After all, they made the mess.

6. Carefully arrange your unguents, devices, and toiletries. Convenience and aesthetics both count. Clean the sink after rinsing your sponge for the last time. Finish by shining up the fixtures and mirrors with the last dry part of whatever cloth you still have available and then toss it in the laundry basket.

Whether you realize it or not, you want your nakedness to be received in a purified enclosure. Yet you are also a busy, modern person with little time for perfection. The best solution is *simple daily maintenance*. This means to wipe dry or squeegee the shower and mirrors after each use. Rinse and dry the sink every day, especially if someone in your house is in the habit of dropping and abandoning globs of toothpaste. If you are really motivated, a quick swab with lemon oil will keep your tile and Formica shiny and sweet-smelling without any scrubbing.

The squeegee is the best invention for saving time in the shower stall, and it has recently become widely available in every bath shop and hardware store in town. Before I even leave the shower, I squeegee the glass door and tile walls and have completely prevented mildew, lime, and mold stains. (Lime-Away works well if you need it, but you won't if you squeegee.) The new shower cleaning products expand on this technique. Spray after showering and you're done. That's terrific, too. It allows you to keep the ritual, without the work.

When you clean out your bathroom and make it all shiny and sparkly, you are telling your body that you are sacred. A dirty temple does not honor its patrons. When the disciple cleans the temple and the temple treasures, she is honoring herself as she honors her Deity. When you enter your bathroom as a sacred purification site, you want it to purify *you*; if it is filthy it will only make you feel wretched. Feeling like a wretch is not what a healing spirituality is about.

As you finish up, look around your temple and find your "altar." You already have one, even if you don't know it. Look for an arrangement of objects that carry a special message about your body's relationship to Spirit. Is this the altar you want in your temple? Is it a pile of dirty clothes growing mildew in the corner? Is it hidden inside the medicine cabinet, looking like a line-up of the usual curative suspects? Is it a Druid circle of scented powders and sprays that give the message you stink? If you haven't made an altar purposely, mundane products that give your temple a mundane atmosphere will take that position. Take the time to make one that reminds you to praise your body's creation by divine principles. Find symbolic objects that speak to your unconscious about its sacredness: candles, soft scents, stones, shells, flowers (dried or fresh), pictures of people or places, real or imagined, that evoke natural beauty and a hallowed air. No, gentlemen, you will not be thought a sissy if your bathroom smells better than a locker room. You will, however, be thought a good catch.

Your "temple" does not have to be the perfect modern bathroom, nor the best design by architectural standards. Nor do you need a lot of money to feel "blessed" within its walls. It just has to meet your basic needs for comfort . . . and then beyond that for blessing.

The bathroom that was my favorite sanctuary was in a Massachusetts flat that did not even have a shower, only a bathtub. This place was so cheap that I paid my rent while cleaning only one house a day for thirty-five bucks each. Granted, I had to closely monitor my hot water usage or I could get caught with a head full of suds and nothing but cold from the tap. But the bathroom was big enough for a multitude of plants, an altar, and a rocking chair, which doubled as a valet. The tub was an enameled cast iron antique with claw feet and long enough to stretch out in. I had a second set of speakers wired in from the stereo. An imitation Persian rug gussied up the linoleum floor, and Maxfield Parrish bathing prints—as ubiquitous that decade as Indian bedspreads had been the decade before and mini blinds the decade after—adorned the walls, complemented by postcards sent by friends all over the world on the cabinet doors.

Next to the tub on a low table I had a vanilla-scented candle and a shell for burning incense. Nestled around several potted plants, I placed small objects special to me, reminding me of qualities of character or ways of being that I valued. These included a tiny brass snake I picked up at an antique store in New Haven, Connecticut that evoked for me the power to change; a perfectly shaped miniature sand dollar from a Sarasota, Florida beach, a reminder of nature's abundance and grace; a red glass marble I'd had with me since fifth grade in St. Louis, Missouri, special for reasons that remain a mystery to me. Also on this table were my Bluebird ring, dry yellow rose petals I kept in a tiny tea cup given me by my grandmother for my seventh birthday, a rubber Gumby, and a robin's egg I'd found in the yard of that Florence, Massachusetts flat. All these things put me in touch with the past, the present, the future, and all sorts of geography. They exuded qualities of stealth, transformation, endurance, and tenacity. Reminded me of hope, passion, compassion, and fun.

These were my own personal spirit fetishes. Some of them I still have. You will have your own. You may want symbols that have broad and powerful meaning for large groups of people, such as religious icons, a Crucifix, a Star of David, a statue of the Buddha, an ankh, and so on. Others are just personal, like mine above. Your altar should be a small area set aside with anything that helps your mind connect to the great qualities that help you live a day: love, courage, serenity, wisdom, flexibility, you name them. Start with the four elements—fire, earth, air, and water. These stimulate your ancient brain through your five senses, reminding you of your auspicious beginnings.

- A candle is a good thing. It represents the heat of drive and desire, and the flickering light in the mystery of clarity. Not to mention the magic it performs on certain indefensible odors.

- The smoke of incense or sage fills the air, also stimulating your sense of smell, the sense that holds the ancient memory. Smoke is also believed to escort prayers to the unseen world of the Infinite.

- In the bathroom you already have plenty of water, the element that represents things like emotion, nurturance, and resilience. Its many uses also invigorate your senses of touch, taste, sight, and hearing.

- Rocks, shells, and feathers bring in the worlds of mineral, sea, and sky. Green plants suggest growth. You can incorporate fabrics as well: for example, silks and satins for abundance, denim for durability and familiarity, velvets and velour for lushness and comfort. My altar was laid upon a sampler of fine needlework sewn in childhood by a woman I once worked for who had become almost a second mother to me. The cloth honored the connection between us, giving me solace.

In that bathroom, when my tub was full, sweetened by a gift of bath salts, the stereo playing Nina Simone, candles flickering vanilla or cinnamon (or, ah sweet plenty, both!), casting shadows of wandering jew and jade across the walls as the dimming light of dusk peeked through my woven wicker shades, and I in need of hope that my dreams would not die without my having had a chance to manifest them, I would call on the power existing in the universe—the power that created fire and light, birth and photosynthesis; that fueled memory and relationship, and made diversity an art and beauty a staple—and I would bathe myself in the knowledge that such power existed in me if it existed at all. Everything in the temple of my bathroom showed how it existed in all things. And I would purify myself of the doubt that tormented me in those dark nights of my soul, which said it couldn't exist for me. And I would anoint myself with the balm provided by the objects on my altar and the decor surrounding me, and with the prayer that I was as deserving as any of these other reflections of the creative life spirit. Then I could prepare to meet the world having communed with the light in the darkness, integrating these great forces within me. Healing *is* possible. Try it on in the bath.

PRACTICE PAGE

Going to the Chapel and We're . . .

The following tasks ask you to wed your continuing inventory process to your body—its life experience, its cravings, and its minimum daily requirements.

The Path of the Body . . .

How well do you know your body? Could you write its autobiography? Could you draw it? Make a list, tell the story, or draw a picture of each and every pleasure, injury, illness, or skill your body has experienced, overcome, or mastered. If you've been told but you don't remember that you had the mumps at age two, include it. If you remember, but you've been told you never did sprain your ankle at age ten, include that as well. You can do this in whatever way you choose: a simple itemized list in chronological order, a meandering story on a tape recorder starting at your feet and moving up your body till you're done, a picture on a sketch pad; in categories of *pain* and *pleasure*, or all mixed together. If you draw it, it doesn't have to be a good likeness—even a cartoon outline of a generic body is fine. Simply declare it yours. Make copies of it, if you want more than one of these. Mark it with symbols that represent each ache, pain, joy, and triumph. Or color-code it. Let your body tell its whole story without judgment. If it was painful but you liked it, fine; if it was supposed to be the greatest thing, but it made you sick, that's okay too. These are the events by which you came to understand your body's capabilities, limitations, and requirements.

. . . Is Paved with Craving

Some people think there is an "addictive personality." I don't know if there is or not, but I do think most of us are addicted to something or someone at one time or another. Something we can't or won't give up because we like it or because we need it. This addiction may or may not be something you had to quit because it made your life "unmanageable." That's not the point here. This exercise asks you to add them up, every one: major, minor, substance, behavior, emotion, or ritual (like how you brush your teeth for example), whatever. Make a list of all the people, places, processes, and things you've ever been addicted to, and annotate them, explaining how they developed, how they changed (if they changed), and how you think they function for your survival, if you still use them. Mark which ones you've quit and which ones you've kept. This way you will be able to look at how you make and break habits. Is there a pattern to the process, or are they each different? You may also want to include the year or the age at which you started and stopped the addiction.

Some will be easier to identify than others: smoking, coffee, and TV are so common they're hard to miss, while qualities like perfectionism, love, and structure (or the lack of it) are more hidden, though equally inimical to disruption. Some are good for you in moderation: flossing, journaling, jogging; some are dangerous when overdone: alcohol, drugs, work, religion, sex, food; and others when underdone: grooming and again, food. An addiction needs disruption if it is causing problems with your life or health management. But it's good to be aware of everything you use to manage your stress or to alter your consciousness, whether you feel you must quit it or not.

This you can draw as well. Take your picture from Exercise 1 or use a new original. Devote a different symbol to each addiction and try to associate it with an area of the body. A cigarette, for example, may be drawn in the hands or in the mouth, or maybe it's in the lungs for you. A bottle of alcohol may belong in the brain or the belly. And so on. Draw a picture of the addiction wherever you feel it connects to you physically. When it's not obvious, use your intuition.

The first time I did this assignment, I was quite surprised at the long list of both dangerous and harmless things I was addicted to. Tea, coffee, time, love, pot. But what really blew my mind was what I neglected to list. Sucking on Newport Lights through hours of writing, I completely left out smoking. Didn't even notice it till I talked about the paper with the acting teacher who assigned it, Linda Putnam (1983–84). Clearly I was dealing with something deep. Or not dealing with it, as the case may be. However, eventually I did do the work and quit smoking . . . everything.

Clean Your Bathroom

Use the method described earlier in this chapter. Set up an altar with personal items that connect you to the spirit of creation or creativity. Light a candle in your "temple" and spend time communing with that spirit.

Bathing Meditation

Repeat the same self-massage and movement exercise from the Practice Pages of chapter 3, using the audiotape if you made one. Only don't stand up this time or move in any way that could cause you to slip, because you're going to do this in a BATHTUB filled with water. *You're soaking in it.* Note any differences in your experience from the last time.

CHAPTER 5

DOUBT AND FAILURE: LOST IN THE MARGINS

... Thought is born of failure. ... Only when the human organism fails to achieve an adequate response to its situation is there material for [new] processes of thought, and the greater the failure, the more searching [humans] become.

—L.L. Whyte, *The Next Development of Man.*
In *The Primal Mind*

If you've lived long enough to buy books on healing, then you already know that change and loss are part of life. In fact, nearly everything and everyone you care about (love, companionship, health, wealth) will—for better or worse, for now or forever—leave you or leave you empty. Only two things are sure to stay by you through thick and thin, and these are doubt and failure. You'd better make friends with them.

When you are in the throes of some great deed or life transition, whom can you depend upon for company? Doubt. When you are enjoying the fruits of your accomplishment, satiated by the congratulations lauding your success, who can you expect to come knocking at your door, bags in hand, all set for a nice long visit? Failure. Or at least the fear of it.

And when you inevitably sink with disappointment, hurt, and worry, your friends having deserted you in your hour of darkness, your family looking at you sideways in judgment, who will stand by you, never leaving you alone for one minute? That's right, your favorite couple, Doubt and Failure. There is not a new job, a longed-for promotion, a creative endeavor, a new relationship, not the purchase of a new home, the advent of children, the saving for an education, not even divorce, no time that these two specters do not appear in the picture.

What do we do with them, then? How do we handle their demands on us? As you would any high-maintenance pal. Let them talk and talk, jabbering on about themselves at length for as long as you can stand it. About how whatever it is you're doing didn't work or won't work. About how you don't really know what you're doing and never did. They like to harp on everything that you aren't sure about. About the part of your life plan that's unclear, unknown, in the dark, hidden. They are very concerned about that dark side of the moon, about what lurks in those shadowed corners. But that's why you keep them as friends; because they are explorers in a way. They are always shining a harsh bright light on your unknowns.

But they are self-absorbed explorers, and finally you must interrupt. Insist they quiet down long enough to let you get back to work on your sacred space. In times of doubt and failure, when things aren't quite working for you, sacred space can seem pretty remote. Like maybe *this* house is beyond the pale. The clutter won't clean up. That stain on the carpet stands out even worse now that the rest of the rug is clean. You've started using the unpacked boxes in the bedroom as end tables. It's not a good thing.

Maybe it's not the house so much as the house*mates*. The people you share your life with—friends, partner, parents, kids—won't get on board. Maybe they're making fun of your efforts, calling it "making *scared* space." Maybe you doubt your ability to change anything about your space, much less your relationships or your life. Maybe sometimes you doubt your will to live. You fear you're going crazy. So, you push that thought away and give it the ol' college try, only to find a really big pocket of crud that you doubt any sweeping or scrubbing will ever get clean. You begin to think you've set yourself up to fail.

Believe it or not, this point marks the real beginning of healing. The house overwhelms you. It might be that doubt and failure operate in your home the same way they operate in your life. Are there "ghetto" areas in your home? Places where you've stashed stuff you don't know what to do with? An undecorated room, a catchall corner, a junk drawer—an area that you neglected "for now," and now has stretched into forever? There is nothing to do at this point but change the way you see.

Blighted areas express parts of you that are still "in the dark," unknown to you; skills that you are unsure of, mistakes that have not yet revealed their lessons, the continually uncertain future. They are the doubts, fears, and failures that make you uncomfortable because they contradict what you tell yourself about adulthood: that you should be confident, together, positive-thinking, that you should know what you are doing, that you should be—in the words of

Henley's oft misapplied poem, "Invictus"—the "master of your fate, and the captain of your soul." Instead, they point out that you do not live up to the image you want to project, much less to the person you want to be. In fact, they illuminate what you need to look at and give extra attention to. They make obvious what needs cleaning up all around.

What you will need to clean up and brighten these areas is a different way to look at them. I wish I could hand the new perspective to you, but I can't. You will have to find it for yourself. But I will tell you where to start: with forgiveness. Forgive your unorganized rooms, your resistant stains, and also your unmet expectations. Let us agree for now to hang in there without judgment, despite perfection eluding your efforts, for no other reason than that these failures are part of your sacred space. Once forgiven, you are free to become as grand as you are. Thus, you stay with your issues, forgiving yourself for being difficult. Now is the time for extraordinary measures.

Houses and Spots That Just Won't Clean

You know you've got these areas: The goop beneath the stove. The muck behind the refrigerator. The crust of burned-on food. The goo of ground-in grease. Rust, mildew, cat and dog stains. Stains on porcelain, linoleum, hardwood, upholstery, and carpet. Okay, it's true—some flaws you will have to learn to live with, others you'll just throw away. But usually, you *can* clean these up—they just require a little creative problem solving.

There are three basic principles for dealing with resistance: *persistence*, *resources*, and *flexibility*. They hold for cleaning spots as well as for healing resistant injuries, inside or out. Let's treat them one at a time.

Persistence

Persistence means elbow grease. Sometimes you have to clean and reclean. Sometimes you have to commit to your hopes and recommit. Sometimes you have to process your feelings over and over again. Practice new habits. Wax the floor and shine it up again. Sometimes you have to ask yourself, "What is sacred to me in this room?" more than once. More than twice. Sometimes you have to keep trying new things to find what works. It's a drag, I know it.

I was born by cesarean section. It wasn't my fault, it wasn't my choice, but I did not have to struggle to be born. I wasn't born really;

I was *removed*. Maybe that's why the difficulties of life have been a shock to me. Still, other things came easy. Grades, sports, friends. If it didn't come easy, I didn't do it. This became a problem as soon as I grew up. I still don't like to struggle. Working up a sweat gives me a headache. It can be an effort just to make an effort. I'm not proud of it. I'm not advocating it. In fact, making the effort is the thing I struggle with on a daily basis. And sometimes the consequences of *not* pushing past the resistance are worse than the pain of the endeavor.

When it comes to healing, you have no choice. There's a song on the radio right now that goes something like, "Why don't you go ahead and kill yourself? Or just get over it." A cynical and cruel statement, definitely, but it describes a frequent dilemma. If you are not going to pursue "getting over it," there is only one choice. But if you're a conscious person, suicide (like homicide) is not a real option, if for no other reason sometimes than you care enough about your partner, your parents, your kids, or your cat to not put them through it. But that doesn't stop everyone, does it? It doesn't stop you unless you understand, even vaguely, that life with all its experiences is sacred. You must find a way to keep it vital, or come back and start all over with new debts to pay.

Sometimes when healing isn't happening, it can be an indication that you don't *want* to be persistent. In this case, the resistance is in you and not in the injury. The house has its parallel. I have been known to avoid certain stains or piles of clutter for weeks before taking an ammonia-soaked sponge to them, before taking a trip to the office supply store for a box of file folders. It is my (incorrect) assumption that the stains are permanent that keeps me from going after them on my hands and knees only to discover they are not stains at all, just an awful mess. Or I believe the piles are essential to my well-being and not just stuff that I don't want to look at. But I finally have to get to it, or be swallowed in the mire. In the same way, when your sacred space and you are ready, you will do your healing work. For most of us, the problems we are living with are only as immutable as we think they are. And we could think again. If you practice moving through that resistance by cleaning something you've been avoiding, it will assist you in finding the part of you that can persist on your own behalf as well.

Let's be clear: Elbow grease does not require lots of muscular effort. *Persistence is the repetition of tiny steps.* Filth becomes a stain-like mess by repeated abuse. It takes repeated attention to clean it up. By repeating light scrubbing motions with a nonscratching sponge, you eventually get through the gunk. Whether you are cleaning black shoe streaks on the floor, ink on the wall, or coffee stains on the upholstery, you'll find that things that seem impossible, aren't. You don't have to take up the linoleum or patch the plaster—the right sponge with the right solvent and the right touch will handle it most of the time.

By the same token, nudging at your doubt and fear with light but repeated suggestions for the right solution will chip away at the sense of failure, lessening the stain left from past disappointments. Do not fear the "black marks" on your character left there by mistakes and hurts. The only stain that is truly impervious to removal is a bleach stain, the one made by trying to whitewash yourself out of existence.

Persistence involves keeping your attention tuned to that which you can change—whether your "darkness" manifests as nightmares, poor eating habits, flashbacks, bad relationships, or destructive work habits. Keep at it until you find your own creative solution, an approach designed just for you. Look for solutions in every avenue of your being: physical, mental, emotional, and spiritual. When one doesn't work, try another. You are looking to change the stagnated energy caused by paralyzing fear, just as you would look to change the energy of a room in chaos. When the energy changes for a thing, it is the beginning of changing the thing. You may need specific help to make that shift. Which brings us to . . .

Resources

A woman I know had what she thought was a spider bite on her arm. It wouldn't heal. She treated it with hydrogen peroxide, Benadryl, and Cortaid. It blistered, got worse, itched, stung, sometimes even ached. For weeks. She was afraid she had flesh-eating disease. When she discovered ringworm on her cat, her growing panic ceased, if not her dismay. It turned our she actually had ringworm. Finally she could treat it correctly and begin the long process of clearing it up. It just goes to show, you have to know what you have to know what you need. It's been said before, and it still holds true: You need *the proper tool for the proper job.*

Stain removers are better than ever—many of today's products actually work, which wasn't always the case. The best answer to stain removal, though, is still to attend to it immediately. Coffee, tea, even blood and wine will come out if you soak the injured item immediately. If you can't do it immediately, then as soon as you can, apply a stain stick like Shout to it and then soak. When you can see the stain breaking up, put regular soap on it and rub vigorously, using another part of the same fabric. Most of your cleaning problems will work out better with immediate application of just plain soap and water. Restaurateurs will swear by club soda, the sodium in it adding a mild bleaching agent to the remedy. However, you must use caution when using any bleach, especially chlorine bleach, of course. Splashing accidents will suck the color right out of the fabric, never to be returned. Eventually it will rot the cloth as well, an object lesson for anyone who thinks whiter is better.

Whatever the blotch problem, ignoring it usually leads to entrenchment. In my travels I have seen sooty kitchen floors that were not really black, just blackened with dirt and grime—sometimes so thick that only a scraper would get through it. That, a *green*-backed sponge, ammonia, and hours of concentrated labor finally revealed that one particular floor was blue, if somewhat dulled. It might take a perfectly well-intentioned person ages to face such a floor. Another would just tear up that old floor and replace it rather than tackle the cleaning. Either practice works.

In the old days we used to say *protein gets out protein* (for example, mayonnaise for blood stains), *acid removes acid* (lemon juice for wine and tomato stains), and *baking soda and vinegar get out everything else*. In those days, everything I owned was stained. Nowadays, some of the new liquid stain and spot removers are fabulous for clothing, upholstery, and carpets, and are widely available in formulas for both water-based and oil-based stains. I like Total Clean 1 and Total Clean 2, manufactured by Ultra Care International of Canada, as well as Whink, available at some grocery and hardware stores. Whatever product you use, always blot with a clean white cloth in a circular motion to avoid transmitting dye or restaining the area accidentally. Be careful also of bleaching a spot where the blot was. Rust stains can be removed naturally from porcelain sinks and tubs with Heloise's favorite mixture of borax and lemon juice (1992) and your trusty *white* nylon-backed sponge.

Sunshine. We all know it fades curtains, floors, and rugs. It also takes out stains. My brother recently visited me with his infant son and impressed me with his bib treatment. After feeding my nephew each of his pureed meals of chicken, peas, or peaches, his dad rinsed out the bib and laid it in the sun on my back patio. In about an hour it was bleached white again. Of course, don't let the item dry before the stain is gone, or you might be cooking it in instead.

The next best thing to Linda Cobb's handbook of stain removal tips, *Talking Dirty with the Queen of Clean* (1998), for specific resistant cleaning problems would be a toll-free number. Guess what, they do exist. With Web sites, too.

- Halbro's Cleaning Solutions
  1-800-645-9520
  http://www.cleaningpro.com

- Don Aslett's Cleaning Center
  1-800-451-2402

- International Distribution System (IDS)
  This research and development company gives only its Web site.
  www.cleaningequipment.com

These companies each offer a complete product line. You might want to formulate your question to get the information you need without the product pitch. However, they may have exactly what you need to solve your resistant spot problem, and you can probably get it by mail order. Some may come with a guarantee, so be sure to request it. Including them here is a convenience only, not an endorsement of any of these sites or companies.

Resistant clutter and organizational problems have a lot to do with a lack of storage space. So say the many books that have been written about clutter. Cassandra Kent's *Organizing Hints & Tips* (1997) and Don Aslett's *Clutter's Last Stand* (1984), are just two with good ideas if you're serious about minimizing it. Plus, entire stores have opened to deal with the stuff, notably the chain, Hold Everything, found in most malls and mailboxes across the country. But what really interests me is the way furniture fashion has shifted to deal with it. From IKEA to Pottery Barn, from the Bombay Company to Restoration Hardware, low-profile home furnishings are now all about arranging our clutter. You no longer have to be a graduate student to use a steamer trunk for your coffee table. You can now spend quite a bit of money for an antique-*looking* one and call it style. Inspired by European use-of-space designs and Depression-era conservationism, these new styles are ingenious and classic—and they work. There are lots of drawers, shelves, and cupboards to present as decor, which will also store your clutter. This furniture actually helps you ration your clutter out, keeping it handy, while keeping it hidden. Hence: decor-rations. As it should be, keeps us from getting too gaudy.

On the other hand, if you lack know-how or patience, Denslow Brown—the "Organizer Coach"—says that you may need "supportive, practical, concrete help." Trained to work with people suffering from attention deficit disorder (A.D.D. or A.D.H.D.) as well as other chronically chaotic causes, Ms. Brown is only one example of the burgeoning growth industry in "practical healing" (Brown 2000).

I only wish that resources for healing could be so accessible and so fashionable. Then you could find them in every mall across the land. Since they aren't, you might have to work a little harder to find those that suit you. Word-of-mouth referral is always the best way, but you can also find them advertised in alternative publications, holistic health centers, and on the Internet. For mental and emotional healing, there are therapists of every stripe: psychiatrists; psychologists; social workers; Marriage, Family, and Child Counselors (MFCC); Certified Alcohol and Drug Counselors (CADC); and pastoral counselors. For physical and organic issues, you can find both traditional physicians (MDs) and alternative medicine practitioners (in modalities ranging from Ayurveda to osteopathy to acupuncture to Oriental medicine, with its use of Chinese herbs) who are more attuned to communicating with (meaning *listening* to) the patient than they used to be. You must take the time to search for the doctor you feel comfortable with. Broadening your approach to include nutritional counselors and body workers will involve your diet, your attitude, the release and balance of muscles, joints, and nervous systems, your breathing style, and visualization into your journey toward optimal wellness, pain management, peace, contentment, fulfillment, and personal transformation. There is something for every preference.

If you are healing from any kind of trauma, whether from childhood or from last week, the more modalities you employ, the faster and more fully you will heal. This is because trauma causes injury to every level of being—mind, body, and spirit. While counseling and pharmaceuticals are getting better at dealing with the effects of trauma, it is important to include body work in the healing plan as well. It will hasten the healing and lessen the emotional impact by releasing what is stored in the actual cells of the body. The modern dance pioneer Martha Graham was renowned for saying to her dancers, "The body doesn't lie." She was right. That's why body work is also the best method of breaking through resistance in healing from any malady.

Here are just a few methods of effective bodywork for physical, emotional, and spiritual injuries and illnesses. It is not a comprehensive list. These are listed from the least invasive methods that use the energy of touch only, progressing to more invasive, meaning the body is moved, the tissue manipulated or punctured.

- Natural Energy Healing (a laying-on-of-hands technique)

- Reiki (a laying-on-of-hands technique)

- Trager (some manipulation of the muscles, rocking of the extremities)

- Zero-balancing (subtle manipulation of joints)

- Pilates-based training (a method of exercising through injuries)

- Alexander Technique (movement awareness)

- Feldenkrais (movement awareness)

- Swedish massage (the classic rubdown)

- Shiatsu and acupressure (massage of pressure points, utilizing acupuncture meridians)

- Heller Work (deep-tissue massage)

- Rolfing (deep-tissue massage)

- Acupuncture (needles inserted at meridian points)

The kinds of resources you will need depend on the inventory you took a few chapters back. What areas of you or your house are in trouble? Is it your body that needs healing? Your emotions? Your mind? Your spirit? Your creativity? Your economics? Have you discovered what you need to have on hand to make yourself feel supported? Do you have these things? What about for uplifting your spirits? If your materials are abundant but your healing is still-resistant, maybe your motivation to heal needs a jump-start. Perhaps you would benefit by the external stimulus of a group to learn about things that work for other people. Maybe you just need the company! It could be a recovery group, a therapy group, or a task-oriented hobby group such as community theatre, or writing or art classes. Check the listings in your community newspaper or holistic healing monthly to help you find a group or practitioner in your area. Again the Internet can help. Some Web sites and phone numbers with links to possible referrals follow.

- The Body-Mind QueenDom at **http://www.queendom.com/index1.html**

- Child Help USA (also lists resources for adults in recovery) **1-800-4-A CHILD**

- American Society of Alternative Therapists at: **http://www.asat.org/**

- Any of the anonymous 12-step programs: AA, Al-Anon, AcoA, MA, NA, CA, ISA, OA, etc. If you find one in your area, you will be led to the others.

An organization's appearance here is not an endorsement—I found these interesting, but you may not. Which brings us to the third principle. . . .

Flexibility

Sometimes you just have to let go of your expectations. Changing the way you *see* can open up whole new avenues to follow that had not appeared before. Several years ago I read what started as a tragic story about a woman who was so seriously paralyzed by a seizure that she was mistakenly thought to be in a coma (Meyer 1995). In despair at their inability to revitalize her, her family and physicians pronounced her terminal and consigned her to minimum custodial care. There she lay on a hospital bed, unable to let anyone know that she was fully conscious and *fully feeling*, just completely unable to move or speak. That she survived the desperate torture of that was almost the greater wonder.

Finally *after six years*, her sister—despite having no medical training, or possibly because of it—began to see subtle signs of consciousness in the stillness. Alone in her hope, she devised an elaborate system of getting questions answered with the slightest twitches of the eyes. It worked. She was able to prove that her sister was not only awake, but completely responsive in her mind, if not in her body, and desperate to communicate her presence. Eventually the patient's life was restored and her mind liberated by the clever contrivance of physical assistance apparatus. A thrilling result, considering that her disability was so horrifying to her loved ones at the outset that the reality of her recovery was impossible to see.

Here's the lesson: Never assign old definitions to new conditions. Before you're sure you're defeated, look for the subtle signs of liberation within you—even if you do not understand these signs.

Being flexible often means giving up on understanding, itself. As "The Serenity Prayer" (Niebuhr 1943) suggests, some things you must simply accept. Of course, there are things beyond understanding—irrational acts against nature and innocence, for example. But even less extreme things occur for no apparent reason. It is not unusual to be baffled at our own behavior at times, much less someone else's. When this happens, give up trying to understand. That leaves room for grace, releasing you from suffering.

If it sounds like I am advocating giving in, just sentences after exhorting you to not give up, let me clarify. Persist until defeat (with a stain or grunge spot, in a relationship, a job, a neighborhood, or a type of therapeutic treatment) is certain. Then accept it graciously and adjust your expectations. Let go of the normal ways you have of perceiving things, thinking about them and taking action. Then let a new way seep in, allow your desire for healing to change its own shape.

Here's how. Chuck it, walk away from it, replace it, cover it up, decorate around it, get used to it, learn to love it, enhance it, enlarge it, tell everyone that's how you always wanted it. In other words, let freedom ring. Let these unchangeable damages become an opportunity for creative action. Or receptive inaction. Find a *new* way to go.

Being flexible means you do not have to take a vacation with an abusive family, for example. Instead you accept yourself as too emotionally sensitive for that kind of immersion, so you don't go. Flexibility means you make other exceptions to the expected course for yourself and others, out of love. If you have kids and dogs, say, you might have to give up on spotlessness. But look what you get instead—life in motion. It behooves you to prefer that.

You and your house can enjoy each other in your imperfect states just as well as if you had reached your ideal life; you can be okay incompletely healed. Some of this imperfection is what gives you—both house and person—character. A sacred space is not a perfect space. Ancient Japanese printmakers said, "It's the imperfection that makes perfection." They made sure the artwork would be flawed in some way. Sacred is a space that holds the lives within it in divine reflection. As we've said, keeping it clean is a good thing. It's sanitation. Accepting the spots that can't be cleaned is *sanity*.

As you search for new solutions in your sacred space, applying extra energy to your cleaning and healing questions, looking twice at your "ghetto" areas to find the fresher view, remember to enjoy the company of Doubt. Watch how she helps and how she hinders. Let Failure put his feet on the couch and relax awhile. Notice how you come back to yourself and the world you used to know. This is the feeling of your spirit falling back into place. Give it time. It is essential that you be patient with yourself especially when patience is hard to find from others. Forgive them, too, they know not who you be.

PRACTICE PAGES

Your Personal Elementary Alternative Resource List a.k.a. PEARL

Often the most valuable resources are the ones that are custom designed for you, by you. But too many of us do not take the time to develop it. This is your opportunity to put together a list of materials and methods that work for you when the doubt and failure moves in, threatening to overwhelm. It's your own special PEARL, culture it and keep it safe where you can find it when you need it. If you've been working the book to this point, some of these you will already have acquired. If not, here's another chance.

The first four start you off with a tried and true method called HALT. HALT is an acronym used by twelve-step groups, reminding people in recovery to stop, look and listen to their needs when things get rough. Its letters mean to stop before you are too **hungry**, too **angry**, too **lonely**, or too **tired,** preventing an emotional emergency situation. These and the rest of the questions will help you elaborate on the kind of low cost, low maintenance help that will work for you.

1. **HUNGRY**. List three foods that are nutritious, easy to prepare, and feel good to eat. These are the staples you should always have on hand. You may also want to list those foods to stay away from because you react poorly to them.

   A. _____

   B. _____

   C. _____

2. **ANGRY.** Do you ever want to hurt yourself or someone else? Admit it, know it, and think of a cathartic alternative. List three nonviolent ways you can release pent-up anger. For example, take some space, write about your feelings, scribble and scrawl on newsprint, call someone, make lots of noise, beat a bathtub with a wet towel. Do dishes.

   A. _____

   B. _____

   C. _____

3. **LONELY.** List phone numbers and addresses of personal contacts for light or deep company. Who can you call? Where can you go?

A. _____

B. _____

C. _____

D. 1-800-4-A CHILD. Adults and children may call for help.

4. **TIRED.** List three restful things in addition to sleep. What activities and nonactivities offer relief and relaxation? Can you meditate, listen to music, take a nap, or draw a sunflower? If you're not sleeping, you need to get rest in other ways. If you are sleeping, you still need alternatives.

A. Sleep! An average of at least eight hours a night. Yes, you do too need it.

B. _____

C. _____

D. _____

5. **MOVE YOUR BODY.** Not just fitness exercises, though that works too, but any physical remedies for releasing toxic emotional energy. For example, take a brisk walk, run around a track, throw darts, play a racquet sport, swim, get a massage, dance, ride your bike, sweep or vacuum your floors.

A. _____

B. _____

C. _____

6. **EXPRESS YOUR CREATIVITY.** What do you have in your house that helps you find your creative ways of expressing? Do you have musical instruments or art materials on hand? If you don't have any, get them—everyone needs them. For example: crayons, newsprint, marker pens, chalk, cardboard, magazines, drums, clay, glue. And use them!

A. _____

B. _____

C. _____

7. **YOUR INNER CHILD.** List the people to whom this little soul would like to write, including yourself. Get some jumbo crayons or markers and, with your nondominant hand, write someone on your list a letter on BIG paper. Ask her/him questions, and tell them what you need. Write the answer you'd like back with your dominant hand.

A. _____

B. _____

C. _____

8. **SAD?** List three things that comfort you. How would you like to be held? Do you have a special (or secret) doll, pillow, or blanket? Hold it, whatever it is, wrap a towel or blanket around you, and rock yourself. Take a bath by candlelight.

A. _____

B. _____

C. _____

9. **SCARED**? List three actions for safety. What makes you feel safe? What makes you feel protected? A song? The TV? Talking to someone? Checking the locks? How does your house make you feel safe? Is there anything more you need to do, such as putting in a security system? (Radio Shack has some affordable do-it-yourself systems.) Burn sage and tell the demons to go away.

A. _____

B. _____

C. _____

D. Call Impact and Prepare, Inc. for Personal Safety. 1-800-345-KICK. It's a self-defense *system.*

10. **HOPES.** List three things that give you hope. Do you believe in a power greater than yourself—God, Goddess, Nature—that can relieve the burden you now carry alone? Now would be a good time to visualize and communicate with a guardian angel or spirit guide. How does your house remind you of hope? Read or write in bed.

A. _____

B. _____

C. _____

11. **A/VOCATIONS.** Songwriter/activist Charlie King sings, "Our life is/more than our work is/our work is/more than our job." The work of creating sacred space includes broadening the range of your participation in life. These lists can help you do that.

A. What do you want to be "when you grow up"? Where do you want to live? How does your ideal life look? Can you let go of thinking you should already be there?

    i. _____

    ii. _____

    iii. _____

B. What places do you want to visit in the world? How would you like to get there? Can you imagine those places by what you have around you in your home?

    i. _____

    ii. _____

    iii. _____

C. What skills or knowledge would you like to have? Have you got any books or resources to help you acquaint yourself with these things?

    i. _____

    ii. _____

    iii. _____

D. What kind of help do you need to move in the directions you imagine going?

    i. _____

    ii. _____

    iii. _____

E. How do you show yourself that you value your values? Does it show in your house?

    i. _____

    ii. _____

    iii. _____

SAFEHOUSE 1

Every good journey needs a stopping place where you can replenish provisions and rest up. That's what the following blank page is for. I call it a Safehouse. A safehouse is a place where any person can go and trust that they will be protected and allowed to rest. These places have existed throughout history for journeyers escaping persecution: this one is a refuge for you as you journey through this book, whether you are escaping anything or not.

If you have been working the book, you have a clean kitchen, a dusted living room, a clean bathroom. You have a PEARL of an emergency procedure set up for emotional upheaval; you've taken an inventory of your house, your life, and your body. You've begun to feed you spirit, nourish your mind, move your body, and gather support. You might have things to say about any number of these things. If you have not worked it, but only read it, what has kept you from doing the Practice Pages? You no doubt have things to say as well. These pages are for you to express them. Here is your chance to write in the book.

CHAPTER 6

IN SEARCH OF
BOUNDARIES: WALLS,
HALLS, FLOORS, AND
CEILINGS

The beginning of everything is nothing. Out of the mystery of nothing, the miracle of everything emerges . . . [but at] this very earliest moment of transformation, nothing moves.

—Master Lam Kam Chuen,
Feng Shui Handbook

Whether your home is tiny or huge, whether your life is highly ordered or completely unstructured, there are times when you pace the hall, unable to focus, when you feel lost at sea in your own space. It can last for just a short while or it can seem like forever. It happens to almost everyone when waiting for someone or something to arrive. You don't know what to do with yourself in the meantime. It's not a serious problem—that's what magazines are for. But if it's happening all the time, it might be because you are waiting for someone or something to tell you who you are. When you don't know what to do with yourself at all, it's a very serious problem. Establishing boundaries is the answer.

Everybody has lost something in their house. You mutter to yourself, "It can't have walked away." Eventually it shows up and you blame it on a poltergeist. But let's say you've lost *yourself* in your house, then what can you do? Maybe you're suffocating from the limits placed upon you, or hiding from internal pressures; or you could be stuck in old definitions of who you are. Maybe you're feeling overwhelmed by the possibilities before you, or by the ones you've missed. Feeling lost in your house is the worst part of feeling lost in your life. It happens when confusion about your place in the world—whether work or home—begins to be a statement about who you are rather than a question. *This is not a fact.* It is a *feeling* of being lost in the void, the proverbial Abyss, where life ends and creation begins.

This feeling—like Alice falling into a rabbit hole, not sure how you got in, much less how to get out—has to do with being out of sync with your internal sense of order, with how the life in your body is managing the frontiers of your time. Maybe it's about work. Are your skills, gifts, and talents finding their expression in a reliable market? Or are you flailing around in jobs and careers that don't fit? Maybe it's about relationship. Do you know who you are with respect to your significant other/s, where you end and the other begins? Or are you searching for your edges in their reactions to you? Maybe it's about transformation, a necessary change that has found this time to push you forward in your life or more deeply into yourself. How comfortable are you not knowing the answers to the sacred questions of your soul? How easy is it for you to not know who you are in work, in relationship, or in your life?

It's not unusual to be confused about your place in the world; everyone goes through it on occasion, even seekers of conscious living, sacred space, or authentic attention. But it's tragic when you become trapped in that confusion. Feeling your way back to a place of comfort with yourself can be a delicate prospect, involving a variety of changes. Relax; lean on the wall. You're going to use it to find out where you are right now.

First, you're going to get a footing on something positive within your being. Then you're going to learn to negotiate your standing in relationship to others, empowering you to know where to lead and when to follow. Once you know your bottom line in these negotiations, you can begin to walk the line from your next step to your wildest dreams. These are boundary issues. And most of us—especially women—have not been taught how to develop them, or how hard to push against them to get somewhere. Believe me, it is much easier to find meaning in your life when you have clear parameters within which to build it. These are represented in your house by *its* parameters: halls, walls, floors, and ceilings.

These structures define your home's boundaries. They create different worlds within the whole by dividing it into separate rooms, worlds joined by doorways, bridged by halls. They are the skin and bones of the house. But by virtue of their structural position, they also represent the *void* of it. Without furnishings in a room, these borders echo in limbo, defining only empty boxes of undefined space—hollow, cold, at once forsaken and confining.

Arrange the furniture aptly, however; set your objects of soul and association around the rooms; put a pot of tea on, and the aggregate of vacant spaces becomes *home*. The walls recede in importance, overtaken by the geography of lived-in space. You walk on solid ground without having to think about it, the ceiling high enough to let you stand up tall. You need these boundaries and definitions to establish the security within which you'll find freedom to grow. Without them, you have an unlivable hull. With them, you have choices about where to place your self.

The walls, halls, floors, and ceilings show you where your edges are. They demonstrate how to connect the loose ends together, and how to leave space to live in the middle. Here physical reality becomes a metaphor for the boundaries and limits you can develop internally, and a model for the center of stability you can duplicate in your surroundings. Working with the infrastructure of your home will give you visceral instruction. When your body understands, your mind will follow.

Talking to Walls, Walking the Floor, and Dancing down the Hallways

If walls could talk . . . would they tell us how to avoid the violations of personal space and public decency they have witnessed? Would they tell us how to hold our heads up though we are battered by winds of change and spoken to like we don't exist? If walls could talk, would they respect our confidences or blab the secrets we reveal when trying to disappear into them, banging our heads in frustration against them? Would they forgive us when we malign their poise, using the phrase: *Just like talking to a wall?* Or do our own spaces really regard us as indifferently as the expression presumes?

In both cases, fearing that walls might report all they've seen and hating them because they don't, we invoke the idea of the edges of the abyss—a feeling of nonexistence that we wish the wall could witness into existence. What if it can? What if you could push on that wall and find your own edges talking back? When there is no one to witness you, let the wall be your witness. Speak clearly—the reverberations will help you to establish your self in reality.

Take a look at your home. Are your walls plaster or drywall? Are the ceilings high or low? Is the floor covered with wood, tile, vinyl, or carpet? If you dreamed these materials, you could analyze the symbolism of the construction. There are some spiritual teachers who say that all life is a dream and each thing encountered sparks with meaning. Bear with me, then, when I ask you to allow these construction materials to tell you about the construction of your personal parameters. Really look at them. This data will tell you about the makeup of your *inner* space.

How are they decorated? What kinds of paint, wallpaper, trim? How are they interrupted? With furniture, pictures, doors, windows? Can you nail into them, or does someone else make the rules? Are they marred with fingerprints and boot marks? What do the switch plates looks like? Are they smudged?

Who cleans the walls (or doesn't) in your house? Who repairs them, puts them up, or tears them down if need be? The more you know about your walls, the more you understand your own sense of boundaries and limits. The more you care for them, the more you understand that personal space needs to be maintained, developed, and deepened.

Let's go in closer. Press against the wall. This is a boundary. Close your eyes and *feel* it. Can you tell by touch if it's plaster and rock hard? Or is it plasterboard, functioning to indicate the boundary rather than enforce it? Look at the details. Maybe it's old and falling down, held up with gluey wallpaper or wood paneling. Or maybe it's got hairline cracks? In what ways does this wall express your own sense of boundaries? How is it different? How well are your own boundaries maintained? If these walls could talk, what would they tell you about your ability to survive in a world of small and large invasions? Talk to your wall. Tell it the one thing you know to be true about where you are in your life right now.

Tools

For small jobs, you'll need a spray cleaning solution and a good sponge.

Additionally, big jobs will require:

- vacuum or dust mop

- two buckets (one to wash, one to rinse)

- sponge mop or large celluloid sponges

- towel to dry

Stains and Smudges

Try these substances if your wall cleaning is mostly about the grime around light switches, doorknobs, and jutting corners:

- **Fingerprints and animal markings:** Use your favorite spray cleaner, your white-backed nylon sponge, and an old toothbrush.

- **On wallpaper:** An art gum eraser will remove many stains. Always test cleaning solutions on an inconspicuous portion of the paper.

    If your wall has borne more serious marks against its integrity, however, try these stronger remedies:

- **Crayon:** Turpentine or other oil-based solvent. Sometimes white toothpaste will work with a scrubby.

- **Ballpoint ink:** Hairspray—and according to the experts, the cheaper, the better—or a mixture of lemon juice and salt.

- **Plastic tape:** Press with a warm iron and use alcohol or nail polish remover.

Rules of Thumb

- Let's start with a controversy. I tend to start at the top because drips are unavoidable and fighting gravity is more than I can take. Others insist on starting at the bottom to prevent making dirty streaks in the first place. It's possible one's preference has more to do with the way your internal boundaries are constructed than with the actual drips. Discovering which you prefer may be very educational: How do you tend to deal with potential mistakes and problems—by allowing for them or by trying to prevent them?

- Don't get locked into one way of doing things.

- If spot-cleaning a smudge on the wall leaves a noticeable clean spot, it's time to wash the entire wall.

- Before you start washing a floor or a wall: Vacuum, sweep, or dry dust to remove all loose dirt, soot, and cobwebs on floor and baseboards, above doors and windows, in corners, and along the ceiling.

- Clean up drips as you go.

- Use two sponges—one to wash, one to rinse—and hold a drying towel over your shoulder, so you can work your way across the wall more efficiently.

One Man's Ceiling . . .

The floor might be said to represent your bottom line, your base rate, the lowest common denominator. These are the limits you won't go beneath. There can be times when you are not able to locate that ground. And then you have to wait for it to rise beneath your feet.

So, you pace. This is the great thing about a floor: It can take it. You can let your legs and all the weight of the world sink into it.

But if your waiting has become procrastinating on your soul's work, then you could be said to be walking the floor like a nervous father waiting for someone else to give birth to your baby. That's old school, you know. Your soul is your responsibility. You will have to refine that floor-walking, as if your life were a department store, with everything you can imagine available to you in it, and you working every counter too. Take charge of both sides of your situation, supervising your practice and supporting your search. This is ground zero, the place where your boundaries and your limits meet.

On the other hand, the *ceiling* represents those things that limit you, the heights that you can't reach above. Much has been written about the "glass ceiling" that keeps women from climbing into the upper echelons of business. There are many unfair limits placed by "society" over certain groups based on characteristics like gender, race, class, disability, location, age, sexuality. If that weren't bad enough, many of us lower the ceiling on ourselves, with our beliefs about our own limitations. Limiting beliefs are certainly influenced by society's ceilings, but, conversely, our beliefs contribute to the power society wields. If we believe the limits are personally true, then the social constraints need only be implied to be enforced. On the other hand, if you don't believe them, you can use your opposing energy to work on raising them. The more who don't believe, the more energy working to raise them.

We don't usually have much individual control or input into our rooms' physical ceilings either. There's rarely anything to clean on them; even the cobwebs are more likely to hang at the edges where the walls are. (An exception to this is the bathroom shower, where mildew, lime, and water stains can often be found on the ceiling. This could be because the "temple" is the most important place to work on limiting beliefs. See how this works?) Every kind of ceiling, literal or figurative, takes a lot of energy to raise, lower, or rebuild. Whether that energy is expended in the form of labor, money, or know-how, it still takes work. But it is not as hard to *finesse* them, to change the altitude they *seem* to be. You can hang things from them to make them more accessible, or light them to brighten their canopy, giving the illusion of raising them. The ceiling is the place where your boundaries and your *limitations* meet.

When you feel grounded, feet firmly on the floor, but free enough to cut a rug, with a ceiling high enough to let you jump for joy, you may be floating around in your life, but you are not lost. To get grounded, you need to be honest about your limits and your limitations.

... Is Another Man's Floor

What has happened in your life that you are powerless over? Such events have presented you with limitations that suggest where you cannot gain strength; thus you have built depth of character and soul instead. This give-and-take between limitations and strengths is among the things that create your infrastructure. Things like circumstances, ailments, injuries, addictions, births, and deaths. For now, let the limitations created by these conditions stand. Accept them as your foundation.

What other conditions exist in your present life that you have *chosen*, conditions that limit you like furniture arrangements limit movement around a room? Things like ideologies, beliefs, people you care about or live in proximity to, jobs, habits. These can be kept, repaired, replaced, or recycled. As you pace the floor, reassess their usefulness to you. Don't take action; just take note. Leaving the void is about identifying the edges of your world and creating enough space to give you room to breathe. Walk your floor with attention to the details in your space. Put your weight into it. Give your body the sensation of your limits and your limitations. Vacuum, or sweep and mop your floor.

- Vacuum rugs and carpets like you would mow your lawn: systematically and in straight rows, leaving no patch undone.

- Mop floors the same way, except the evenness of the row does not matter as much as covering the entire surface. It should dry without streaking, leaving no lay lines at all.

- Move the furniture out of the way and clean the areas beneath it.

- When you mop a floor, use the same two-bucket method—or rinse with running water in the sink—as you would for cleaning walls. There is no sense washing anything with dirty water.

- Be sure to use a no-rinse detergent (most products made for floors are no-rinse) or rinse your soap-washed floor several times. Nowadays, most "no-wax" floors clean up very nicely with a single product, which strips, cleans, and waxes. Wood floors are best mopped with oil soap such as Murphy's Oil Soap, unless the floor is finished with polyurethane, in which case a damp mop does the trick. You can use products like Windex (that's what my hardwood guy tells me) and Endust sprayed on a dust mop if you like it real shiny, but the floor can get slippery. Use good judgment and check the directions of your cleaning products regarding the proper use on your particular floor.

- Include the baseboard *every time* you clean the floor.

Feel the floor holding you—all your weight, the burdens you carry, the things that drag you down. Feel the ground rising up beneath your feet.

Down the Hall, First Door on Your Left . . .

Hallways are for tripping the light fantastic. They are the bridge and the tunnel, pathways, passageways, inroads. The hallway is the room that is a *way*, a viaduct. It gets you to another room. Another world. In your self, halls relate to the corridors between different parts of you. They can integrate you nicely into one whole. Or they can fail to do that. They represent *process.*

They are akin to the neuropathways laying tracks of your experience and perceptions in the grooves and folds of your brain. They slide your consciousness from one area of function to another. When you are lost, perhaps you've fallen into an unfamiliar groove. Keep going and you are sure to land someplace friendly again. Make the way a trip and a half—by paying attention to how you get from here to there.

Working with the halls in your home can give you an opportunity to better develop your understanding of and relationship to the boundaries *within* you that separate one part of you from another. It can tell you something about how you get from one feeling or mood to another. It can open up ways to think about how you can get to a new place in your life that you currently feel cut off from.

Children and cats know all about hallways. To them, they are playrooms for speed, height, sliding, and sneaking up. Children are developing so quickly, they don't have time to question whether the process is right and they have no interest in slowing it. The results have such clear rewards. As for cats, well, with their nine lives and that abundance of curiosity, they are all about luring us into the search. We fearful adults could stand to follow these teachers down hallways a tad more.

Your inner hallways will link you to your past and present, to your healthy, evolved parts, as well as to your undeveloped and fixated parts. Cleaning the hallway mindfully helps you clear out the cobwebs of the corridors in your mind, which will transport you out of the void into terrain that is either familiar or new, depending on what your growing soul needs at this time.

Some people seem to lack these inner corridors. You probably know someone whose parts are hopelessly compartmentalized. Perhaps you know someone—man or woman—with a hunger for passion and intimacy but at the same time a distrust of all attachments. So many people can't see that their inability to connect their world to another's is the root cause of their loneliness. Likewise, when the disparate parts of your own being live in separate rooms with no connecting corridors, and no phone line between them, then there is no way to get from one aspect of yourself to another. If you're also tripping over stuff parked in your hallway, it could indicate that you are tripping over other obligations to yourself as well. If your halls are long, dark, and stark, chances are that's also the way you're feeling about your life's journey. By now, you know the drill: Clean up your relationship to them by cleaning them in your home.

The hall, of course, is only made up of more walls and floors and ceilings, interrupted by openings and closings (exterior ones may even lack the walls or the ceiling). Clearing and cleaning them is simply an intensified version of what you already know, except for the fact that they tend to collect more dust bunny trails. I'll leave the metaphor and symbolism of that situation to your own whimsy.

As you practice your upkeep on these walls, floors, ceilings, and hallways, pay particular attention to the way the wall holds its position, the way the floor affects the stability of the furniture by its evenness, the way the halls feel with, and without, light or air in them. These activities will help you "feed" your own boundaries, understand your limits and limitations, and teach you how to increase the comfort level in your process of finding your way to who or where you want to be.

Nothing Wrong with Wallflowers

Decorating the walls is important. A room can feel bigger or smaller with pictures, mirrors, or curtains. It can feel warmer, *homier*, and more welcoming, while at the same time establishing the appropriate atmosphere. Inside, blank walls feel cold and barren unless they are enlivened by the decorative use of paint. Outside, blank walls invite graffiti or, worse, advertising. On the other hand, art that provides color, shape, or story gives a room a purpose, an identity, and can provide a feeling of belonging or remind you of the fullness in your life. I use the walls to remind me of what's important in my life. A hand drum made in Taos. A framed cover of *The New Yorker*. A favorite artist's paintings. A mirror to remind me I exist in real space.

Similarly, adorning your own personal boundaries with charm, decorum, and values makes you more pleasant and more clear in your transactions with others. It gives a message to other people about what kinds of interaction they can expect to have and that which is expected of them. Obviously, this is easier said than done.

All work with boundaries will teach you about limits and limitations since the walls touch both floor and ceiling. *Limits* are those things you will not give or do; *limitations* are those things you *cannot* give or do—for whatever reason. Knowing them will tell you how to proceed. For example:

- Walls with flat paint are harder to clean than ones with satin and glossy paints. Your best bet is to limit yourself to spot-cleaning.

- Wallpaper can usually be washed much as you would a regular painted wall, but you must take care not to soak the paper through.

- Some wallpaper is better off just vacuumed regularly. When it gets too dingy, the walls need to be repapered.

- Textured walls and ceilings may as well be repainted—you can't clean them. Your sponges and cloths will disintegrate on the rough surface and the wall will not look clean.

In other words, if your boundaries are too hard to maintain because of your limits and limitations, you might need to remake them. Personal boundaries can be redrawn and resurfaced by clarifying your values. How do you identify your limits? Metaphorically speaking, by understanding the purposes of each room and each wall, by accepting what you can't do or can't give—whether because of a temporary or permanent "weakness" or because of a choice out of strength. Walk the floor with your heart and mind awake.

A Note on Windows

Of course we do them! Boundaries are great, but you need to be able to see through them, to open them up to get fresh air, and to get out in case of a fire. So you see, nothing is airtight. In fact, as people say, if a person's eyes are windows to the soul, then a person's windows are the eyes of the house. Keeping them clear is a must and not as bad as it seems.

You can cut down on messy, soggy cleaning if you *vacuum* the windows every time you vacuum the floor. Yep, I said vacuum the windows. Dust is a big part of the dinginess of windows . . . not only on the glass, but also on the screens. Keep them free of dust with the lovely dust brush attachment and you won't be up to your elbows in glass cleaner very often.

When it's time to clean them for real, I have only three words: ammonia, ammonia, ammonia. Use my favorite Yankee spray solution (see chapter 2) if you can't stand the smell of straight ammonia. Use a bucket to rinse out your sponge; use a small squeegee widely available at bed and bath stores; use paper towels or clean newsprint. Avoid the sun or work fast. That's it. Getting the backside of a conventional window is getting easier than it used to be. One suggestion is to mix dishwasher soap with Jet Dry (an automatic dishwasher additive) in a spray attachment for an outdoor hose. Spray the windows one section at a time and rinse with clean water. The water will sheet off just as it advertises for dishwashers: "No spots!" (Chapman and Major 1991). There are new products especially made for exterior windows that promise to do this as well; these are becoming more and more available at grocery and hardware stores. Better than a ladder and a pole any day. A word of caution: Make sure *before* you start spraying your windows with the hose *a)* that they are closed and *b)* that they don't leak; or you could end up with water *inside* your exterior wall.

Things to Think About While Wandering Lost in your Sacred Space

Close your eyes and see what this no-place looks like. The Void, the Abyss, this Nothingness. It is at best oblivion, at worst a dark maze. You are required to surrender. To let go. All the old stuff you were so sure you needed to stay afloat didn't work. Let it go. Bend your knees and lower yourself to the floor, to the planet. Or, slide on over to the wall or the door jamb and lean into it. All of this is part of the planet too. Wood, rock, gypsum. Let gravity take you and your burdens. Accept what you cannot do. Accept what you can do. You can stand on the floor; you can lean on the wall. You can walk, crawl, or run down the hall and back again. Reach into the void and grab the line that attaches to your spirit. Cry for a vision, for a song, for your connection. Listen for your boundaries echoing back in the labyrinth. Wait for sense and sensation to return in familiar ways. In new ways. Talk to the walls. Walk the floors. Listen to the resonance in your heart and dance down the halls—wherever they take you. Name the rooms, the years, the things you will and will not do in the world, the things you can and cannot do for yourself, for others. While you are floating around in nowhere, sweep and mop and wash until you find yourself in place again. You may not know it, but your house is coming together, a sacred space for the whole of you.

PRACTICE PAGES

Self-Knowledge: A Moving Meditation Series

These exercises will provide opportunities to develop your ability to listen to yourself and your environment in order to find or forge your boundaries.

Embracing Your Losses

1. *Sinking into the Floor.* After you've vacuumed and/or mopped your floor, lie down on it, placing a pen and writing pad in close reach. If the floor is too hard or if you have back problems, cushion it with a mat or blankets, and support your knees with a pillow. You can add music to the mix if you wish. Take a minute or two just breathing and feeling the floor beneath you. Let the air wash over the surface of your body. Allow your floor to take the weight of your head, the full bulk of your flesh and bones, and the gravity of your worries; let the burdens of your spirit sink into the foundation. Do you feel yourself grounding or floating? Just notice it. Feel your whole being submerge into the floor, beneath the floor, into the planet itself. Notice if any parts of your body, your joints for example, are uncomfortable or tense. Make any adjustments you need to make. You may want extra pillows under your head, your lower back, feet, arms, or knees. Do not suffer through this exercise.

   Lay there for at least ten minutes, longer if you can. Notice the feelings and thoughts and sounds that float through your consciousness. Censor nothing. If you get nervous or scared, structure the meditation by putting your awareness into your body. Begin at your toes, your feet, your ankles. Work your way up the body, filling in and filling out your whole body with your breath and your awareness. Notice how your thoughts emerge as you put your body together in its wholeness. Jot down your thoughts in short notes. "Bunion" ... "Birds" ... "Jim, age 3" ... "Knee squeaks" ... "Oil change" ... "Left hip's asleep" ... "Hungry" ... etc. Whatever thoughts light, let them come, write them down. Let them go. When the time is up, write a list poem or paragraph using the words you have written down. Begin with the phrase, "On my planet I know _____." Go.

2. *Leaning on the Wall.* Do the above exercise again the next day, but this time sitting against the wall. You may use a chair, but make sure your feet are on the floor. Let your breath send any anxieties and tensions through your feet to the floor, into the floor, to the center of the earth. As you inhale, imagine you are pulling up the warmth and power at the center of the earth back through your feet and into the center of you. Continue for ten or more minutes, once again filling your body with your breath and mind, jotting down stray thoughts, sensations, and feelings as they pass through you. When you are finished, write again using the words you have collected, beginning with the phrase, "My world fills me with _____ ."

    Vary these meditations in any way—lying, sitting, or walking—and use them whenever you want to reconnect your being to the planet that supports you. Honor all that you know and what you are filled with, whether it brings you pleasure or pain. And then let all that go to allow yourself the room to find out more of what there is to know of your soul in the world. If you honor all that you are, know, and feel, your range will broaden until your experience includes plenty of joy. The joy of being completely you, completely alive.

Gettin' Pushy

1. *Shadow Dancing with the Walls.* While you dust or wash your walls, press your palm against the flat wall, just touching. Feel the temperature and the flatness, smoothness, or roughness of the wall against your skin. Now, keep your hand in the same position and back away from the wall just slightly, keeping your eye on the shadow of your hand on the wall. Adjust the light in the room if your body does not cast a shadow, so that it does. Set the light so that the edges of your shadow hand are sharp and clear. Move so that more and more of your body casts its shadow on the wall. See your body's contours. See that this body, this being, is not nothing. See that you are not nothing. See that it is somewhere: here. See that you are somewhere. Here. Hiding in that shadow somewhere is your forgotten and feared monster. Your half-beast. You may wrestle with it, and with all the demons within you. But it won't do to slay it, since it is an essential part of protecting your boundaries. This is the part that knows what you have forgotten about your life and about who you are, the rest of all that your soul is, both the lauded and the reviled. This is the part that fights for you when you stop fighting with it. Dance with the shadow, the angel and the beast on the wall.

2. *Attaching Yourself to a Tether.* In the Greek myth of the Labyrinth and the Minotaur, Ariadne gives Theseus, her forbidden lover, a ball of thread to find his way home after locating and slaying the beast that had been created by her father, the oppressive king. The symbolism should speak to anyone lost in the house of a confusing life partially set up by adherence to rules made by others. We all could do with a lifeline of true love to help us find our way out before we get eaten by the monsters who live there with us. And I'm not talking about the neighbors' kids. I'll tell you what—you do have that lifeline. It is in your own breathing, and the sound you make when letting it out.

What is the word that wants to be spoken as you dance with your shadow? Move that word with sound out of your mind, with your voice, through your heart, out through your arms, your palms, and back into the wall. Let the knowledge that wall holds about strength and stability connect with the skin and bones of your body. Ask any questions you have for the wall, the shadow on the wall, and the monster in the shadow, questions about parameters and limits, beliefs and ideals, values and infractions, edges, margins, beginnings, endings, surroundings. Questions about separations and detachments, attachments and connections. Sing them, chant them, shout them, or if you're too shy, write them down. Touching that wall, now lunge and push, listening for the answers; listen for as long as you've danced and talked. You are following the thread back to the lighted room and yourself. Breathe.

Write your experience down in your journal or share it with another person. Preferably both.

CHAPTER 7

DUNGEONS, DRAGONS, AND BASEMENTS: PARENTS IN STORAGE

In dimness we come slowly down the stairs, gooseflesh on our arms, into the spotlight. The movement of the bulb illuminates our faces, all faces, no longer familiar. We step off the last of the wooden stairs and someone in the kitchen notices we've left the basement door open and closes it, and the square of sun disappears.

—Sallie Teasdale, "The Basement"

Now that you have good boundaries, you are ready to deal with your family, yes? And now that you've found your soul's edges in the structure of your house, you're ready to deal with the skeletons in your closets, right? Ready or not, we're going to forge ahead, so hang on to your hat. If, on the other hand, your efforts to feel your way out of lost space have you hitting the cold hard bottom, then you're already where we're going. We're going to the bottom of your house to clean out the basement.

This group of rooms—basement, attic, closets off the garage— these are the places we warehouse all the stuff we keep even though we can no longer use it. The stuff Aslett's *Cleaning Encyclopedia* (1993) calls "semi-active." This is stuff you don't pay any attention to—you don't protect it from decay or ruin, nor from pests and dry rot, but you expect it to be okay without you. Does that sound familiar? It's sort of how a lot of parents look after their kids, isn't it? Even if yours took better care of you than that, we still associate the basement with the stored memories of childhood. Your own children's memories will likewise recede into this underground realm of the subconscious, shelved until their memories of you start rattling their chains on the pipes once again.

To be sure, there are more familiar associations with the basement. Namely, the imprints of the underworld: dungeons, demons, dragons, devils, and death. You can't deny the architectural similarities to a dungeon—cement floors and walls, sealed high windows that leak nonetheless, creepy crawlies, and the eerie sounds of a furnace: creaks, bangs, and groans of expanding and contracting metal, the sudden roar of flames, the humming of vents and pipes carrying forced hot air. So isolated from the rest of the house, you could be forgotten down there. Sounds just like Dante's Inferno. Very Goth. Every family has a teenager who wants to live down there. Usually it's the one carrying a torch for some denied truth.

No coincidence. Let's not forget that our Judeo-Christian Hell is the domain of the fallen angel, Lucifer, whose name means light-bringing. Without even looking at the countless stories from cultures not as afraid of the dark as ours—and there are plenty, including our own ancient world roots, which point to the Underworld as *the* place of transformation—we can see even this netherworld is poised to bring light if and when its prisoners choose to reconnect with their Divine Source. That light is burning in the torch of what you can't let go of, but don't want to see. So, of course, we're going to pull out all the junk stored in your underground storehouse to see what important messages about where you came from are buried there, that will help you plot where you're going. A fitting, if macabre pun.

Do You Even Know What's Down There?

Somewhere inside that archetypal underworld lurks your lost childhood. Maybe you had some firsts there in those subterranean spaces. Your first kiss. Your first out of breath, ecstatic, terrifying, surprising full-body hump. Maybe you got groped against your consent. Maybe worse. This place speaks in the languages of both indulgence and injury. Persephone's world, the basement is the place of initiation, whether chosen, fortuitous, or forced. The sad fact is that in addition to their customary employment as laundry room, workshop, and rec room, basements are also notoriously common locations for sexual and physical violations for the same reasons they are so enticing—their darkness, insulation, isolation, and infernal atmosphere. Basements, themselves, might be found stored in the bottom of your psyche.

If you don't have one of these caves in your home, you may be thanking your lucky stars, but don't, because it just means your storage problems are elsewhere—the attic, maybe. If the basement is the underworld of physicality, then the attic is the unsnapped mind, the disassociated upper world. Attics have long represented the bats in one's belfry; one's private madness that punishes with emotional turmoil and social exile. Like Bertha Rochester, the mad first wife imprisoned in the attic of Charlotte Brontë's 1847 novel *Jane Eyre*. The early twentieth century writer and economist Charlotte Perkins Gilman exhorted all creative women to kill that mad, repressed woman locked upstairs in one's own brain. More recently, novelist Jean Rhys (1966), in the *Wide Sargasso Sea*, suggested she be set free, having gone mad to begin with because of personal submission and social repression.

Of course both places have a flip side. The basement and attic also house the freely explored imagination. We have the image of young kids like *Pollyanna* dressing up in Nana's attic trunk-stored clothes. Or C. S. Lewis's forgotten attic wardrobe in *The Narnia Chronicles*, which opens through to a magical world. Great fun and bad science exploded from the basement of the wacky family in the play and film of *You Can't Take It with You*. For me, these places meant absolute privacy, providing the liberty and the location for the best times with my siblings early on, and later . . . well, that's my secret.

Then there's the garage, traditionally Dad's venue. And also the port of personal freedoms: the automobile, teen privacy, making out in the rafters, drinking under the workbench, suicide by exhaust. Obviously, these funhouses are potentially dangerous, loaded areas. Lots of folks understandably carry baggage related to them as well.

It's no wonder people avoid cleaning storage rooms. I mean, what if there's a demon down there? It might be a member of the family or something else you don't want to know about. The dirty laundry is often washed in the dingiest room. And if there's a dragon, you may find it's some opportunity you missed, a choice you made for security or approval that now leaves you with a life too tame to sustain your soul. But these are fears, not predictions. More than likely you're going to find enough of both to give you important information, which will advise your choices in the future. The good, the bad, and the ugly—these came together to make the beautiful you.

The basement holds both the wisdom and the want of your "primary judges," a term used in theatre training to describe the original authority figures that reside in your subconscious, usually your parents or other powerful figures from your childhood (Putnam

1983–84). Whether you continue to respect these folks or have rejected their positions entirely; and whether the judges in your brain bear any resemblance to who the people are today or who they ever knew themselves to be, you will find them thriving still as judges in the timeless present of your core foundation. Or, if it's an attic that stockpiles your stored stuff, hanging relentlessly over your head. You have the choice to rot in the dungeon, chained to these skeletons of the past, or to sweep out the cobwebs and set the records straight, honoring their gifts and evicting their ghosts.

Banished to the Downs

And where we had thought to find an abomination, we shall find a god; where we had thought to slay another, we shall slay ourselves; where we had thought to travel outward, we shall come to the center of our own existence; where we had thought to be alone, we shall be with all the world.

—Joseph Campbell, *The Hero with a Thousand Faces*

Separation from parents is not done in a day. It's supposed to take your entire childhood (during which time you're simultaneously bonding with them), and most of your twenties (during which time you're asking for money). Even in the best of families, this doesn't always happen. It is an odd turn of events that, except for the money, both bonding with and separating from parents is happening less and less.

When there is insufficient bonding, rebellion is the only choice for separation. Mind you, rebellion is not the same as individuation. It is more a mirror-image attachment to the source. You attach yourself in an intimate pose as the parents' opposite; whereas, authentic separation-individuation is almost a reconciliation as equals. It's a détente between what was given and what is wished for; a handing-off of ownership of the self from the small "s" source to the capital "s" Source, from parental custodian to sacred autonomy. Letting go of them by letting go of those unselected parts of yourself that are they and not you.

You are chained to the dungeon if you are attached to "what they will say," as much as if you are stuck in "what they did to me." Outdated messages about who you are and what you can be or do with your life are like a prison sentence for as long as you are stuck there. How do you escape? How do you detach? It's a process that begins by identifying what you've stored and then deciding what you want to keep. This is the work of therapy and much of body-work and energy healing therapies. "Body psychotherapy," an emerging field, focuses specifically on the stored messages from the past locked in your body. You can get a jump on it by using the practice of cleaning the basement.

You're going to be sorting, purging, and reorganizing. These are the same activities counselors use for therapy: You sort the feelings out, release the false messages, and reframe your memories with a new perspective that allows you independence. Going through the stuff you've saved for years in your basement will bring up memories and feelings galore. This time, don't muscle through the chore; do it with your mind wide awake.

Keep a notepad handy and make notes of the things that come up for you. Just as you will arrange your things in what the helpful book, *Organizing from the Inside Out* (Morgenstern 1998), calls "ZONES," arrange your thoughts into categories as well—Family, Peers, Partners, Ambitions, Intentions, etc. Subdivide them if you want to. Or make a list of feelings: Anger, Sadness, Gladness, Fear, etc. Chart them on a scale of 1 to 5, annoyance to rage, disappointment to despair, etc.

Jot down a word or a phrase about feelings and memories that arise with each box or piece or cobwebbed corner. Associate the thing with the memory/feeling. Watch for the patterns that emerge from the stuff, both external and internal; note the preponderance of negative and positive attachments. Are there ages or events, locations or individuals that stand out? Are there lies and regrets? Are there missing parts of you waiting for rediscovery? Keeping a multi-leveled list will help you sort your stuff with your stuff. So to speak.

As you sort, look for the dungeon items—the stuck places that reveal the ways you serve old and outdated messages about yourself and your abilities, or the world and your place in it. The process of replacing those messages with useful ones begins with identifying them.

And also look for the dragons. I'm going to suggest you look at these as the beasts you slew in order to get reward from others. Your fears and your phobias; but also your imagination, your wildness, your dreams. These items are the ones that bring chaos to the space. They are things that are not easy to store and forget. They stick out. They remind you of roads not taken, for better or worse. Maybe that bicycle is a dragon. Maybe the folder of poetry. Maybe the collection of broken teacups. Or the blue ribbon from the science fair. Maybe it's your partner's or your kids' stuff that brings up the dirt in you. Take notice and make note of it.

Zen and the Art of Cleaning House

So, let's clean the basement. I understand it might be scary down there. Dark, damp, cut off from the rest of the house, it might seem a Herculean task to remake these dungeons of storage into sacred space. But every temple has its tomb. In fact, the unwavering reach into the darkness for the seed of light buried there may be the most sacred act any temple adept could undertake, spiders and webs notwithstanding. Cheer up, I offer you the 3 P's: Pace, Purge, and Persistence.

Pace

This means take your time. Think before you throw. The main challenge in any storage cellar is organization. Organizing sets your pace. Be prepared to deal with questions that go to the core of your storage issues. Keep an eye on your feelings—they provide the answers to your questions. Take notes.

Questions like: Is your organization a sham? Do you know what you think and feel? You can tell by the ease with which your stuff hangs together. Can you move in and out of your basement, retrieving things and putting them away with a personal logic that is easy for you to remember and repeat? Or are items crammed and abandoned here and there with no relationship to one another? Are related things stashed in opposite corners? Does it just *look* cleaned up, but actually you don't know where a damn thing is or where a new thing goes? Are you someone who hates to see the facts if they disturb the lies you've lived by? Reorganizing will cut down on the hell of maintaining. Once you put your primary authorities in perspective, you will know better how to regard them. Start by clearing off the stairs and putting away the stuff that has been waiting for a saturation point. We'll just assume critical mass has been reached.

How do you feel? Pacing means you can take breaks as you need them or break up the job into different days or different weekends. Take a break if the encounter takes a toll on your psyche. Step gingerly out of the piles of yesteryear and surface upside. Allow yourself to feel. Breathe some fresh air. Blow your nose. Drink a gallon of water. You are not only breathing a lot of dust and dust mites, mold and mildew, but you are traveling back in time. You need to keep your body flushed and your spirit refreshed. Drink lots of water and take plenty of air breaks. Put on an old record. Put on a new CD.

While you're upstairs, load up on supplies: towels, sponges, your trusty spray cleaner, Kleenex, music, a portable telephone. As you reenter your roots cellar—which by now may feel like an old whine cellar—think of this Yankee saw: *A place for everything and everything in its place*. If this gives you flashbacks, scream and click your heels three times, visualizing your favorite place, repeating "There's no place like home...." Thank God for that. Break over.

Purge

After sorting your good, bad, and ugly, it's time to start throwing away your utterly useless. Do you really need to hang onto this stuff? Ask each new or old thing to justify its existence. Certainly tools, laundry, and emergency kits are self-justifying. Perhaps, too, are out-of-season clothes, memory-sheltering photo albums, even crates with files of mementos. But what about that broken garden hose? The hammer with a handle that slips off with every third good whack? The work boots with cracked soles? Please, the sentimental value of some things needs to be reexamined. Rule of thumb: If it's broken or three years have gone by without using it, wearing it, or even thinking about it, get rid of it. Wouldn't it be wonderful if the same could be said for broken promises, unused suggestions, worn-out admonitions, and hand-me-down limitations? Good riddance to bad rubbish.

Check it out. Didn't your saving graces already save you? The caramel-colored teddy bear with the rubbed-off nose, the silver six-shooters with the plastic pearl handles, your favorite blue work shirt, your well-loved peach blanket with the tiny roses, Dad's worn-out tools, Mom's copper teapot, your leotard from your first ballet class, your bantam Rawlings baseball glove worn in with Neetsfoot Oil and line drives. Their work is done. You lived. Honor that. Feel free to commemorate it or give it away. Both are sacred gestures honoring the Universe's recycling plan.

Then there's the other stuff. The stuff you never want to see again but you've appointed yourself curator of. Whatever did happen, you did not die. And then there's the new stuff you've collected on your own. Would it kill you to purge this stuff?

My "basement" has moved from a back porch to a garage as I've moved from an apartment to a house. There are few actual basements in southern California and while I have helped clean some out, none have belonged to me. Consequently some of my precious storage—a box or two of pictures and papers mostly—is in the house, scattered among several upper closet shelves. That stuff is obviously the Chosen. Somehow it tells me where I've been and who I am. I don't want it to be compromised by mildew, dust, and mice—things I can't keep out of my garage. But this chosen stuff isn't current at all, and it doesn't fit into my file cabinets or bookshelves. I rarely look at it, but I feel a sense of history just knowing it's there.

Seeing the box labeled, *Archives: pics and memories,* works like short-hand, running me through the transcripts of my watersheds.

But the rest of the garage is always in flux: garden stones, sprinkler heads, cans of paint in varying shades of white, boogie boards, art materials, skis, wetsuits. Old accounts. The clutter expands and contracts—mostly expanding—as the seasons change, as our time allows for "keeping up on it." In short, as life happens in the areas surrounding the storage spaces. I think it might be the more life you have going on in your home, the more inconstant your storage spaces are. That's okay.

Before we moved in here, the types of questions you are now asking swarmed us: Do we keep the surfboard, even though your neck injury pretty much ended the future of surfing? How about my stepmother's handcrafted Christmas wreath? What about those boo-gie boards? And the extra set of dishes? Turning forty definitely affected both the type of questions and the resistance to answering them. When you change through age or experience, your relation-ship with your stuff changes. But it can take awhile. In the end, the surfboard went, the boogie boards stayed, and *everything* my step-mother handcrafted got pitched. The dishes are waiting for a hypo-thetical summer cottage.

These are the kinds of questions cleaning out the basement brings up. It's important to make them conscious. This way the ghost parents get out of the shadows so you can become the lead actor—the star—of your own life. To be or not to be who you are now, at this time, is a basement dilemma. Because that's where your distant and recent past waits in the wings for the next cue, for the choices you will make that lead to the triumph in the third act.

Persistence

Persistence comes up again, doesn't it? Well, that's how persis-tence works. It repeats itself. And I will repeat that if you are just reading this book and not working it, you're missing out. Do the work as you go through it. Do it now. Don't give up.

You may find you're rearranging, repacking, and purging again and again. Don't worry about it; the basement is never completely cleaned up. Neither are relationships with parents and family, for that matter. You have to revisit your stuff until it ends up in the right place. Things that associate with one another will pile up together. These are Morgenstern's natural "ZONES," mentioned above. The fins and goggles in the beach bag—put them near the boogie boards. Survival gear goes with camping gear. Batteries nearby in a water-tight container, alongside candles, matches, flashlights. Paint, paint thinner, stain, and Spackle together, away from dried food and water packages. And so on. Sounds dumb, it's so simple, right? That's so you don't have to think about it when you go to look for it. As your piles dwindle to the petty stuff, you will find that associations are harder to make, which means these items run the risk of getting lost. So take time now to prevent that. That's where persistence comes in.

If you're saving it, whether it's a memento or a memory, clean it up. It will rot or grow legs if there are secret things left attached. If you've been paying attention throughout this book, this may seem like a *déjà vu*. You're in the basement; the whole thing is a *déjà vu*, don't you get it? Once it's clean it will not seem so creepy.

Cleaning out the dungeon is not for wimps. If you feel wimpy, go slow and it will pass. When you're done, neither the basement nor your parents will intimidate you quite so much. Your issues with your parents sorted and piled, your harvest drying for a long cold winter; purge when you're ready. The key is maintenance, keeping yourself current with your *stuff*. The time spent foraging in the base-ment—airing out the dungeon, reconsidering the dragon, clearing away that which is unnecessary, purging what you thought you needed to lug around, but don't—is the time in the darkness that you need before you can lighten up. It is the housecleaning equiva-lent to ceremonially washing your feet. You've cleansed the founda-tion of where you live.

The Path of the Hero: It's Kind of Complex

[T]he work of the hero . . . is to slay the tenacious aspect of the father (dragon, tester, ogre king) and release from its ban the vital energies that will feed the universe. . . 'This can be done either in accordance with the Father's will or against his will. . . .'

—Joseph Campbell quoting Coomaraswamy,
The Hero with a Thousand Faces

You have to have death in order to have life . . . [There must be a] sacred killing [of] every generation . . . in order that the next generation can come.

—Joseph Campbell, *The Power of Myth*

After you've dealt with all this storage, it can feel as if your life has passed before your eyes. And in a way, it has. When you face these boxes, you face the creators of your being. If you wonder why you seem to give your parents too much power over you, consider that your cells think your parents are God. After all, your very DNA was theirs first. And everyone knows if you're looking at God, you're facing your death.

This *is* the heroic journey, the same journey that sent the orphaned Oedipus on his adventure of the road, only to encounter a stranger determined to block his way. Oedipus killed the stranger and became king after meeting and marrying the isolated queen. Years later he was informed by a sort of keeper of archives that the man he'd killed had been not only the former king, but his natural father. Horrified, he faced his wife and knew they were mother and son. His punishment was swift, self-inflicted, and severe. Today's hero/ine would be furious at the deception, the abandonment, the double tragedy of incest and patricide by a tyrant and an accident. It's time to reread the story as a predictable outcome of neglect and abuse, induced by both parents' need to control their own destiny by controlling their descendant's reality. Oedipus was duped and robbed of his life, but you needn't be. Your cells are your own. The era of blaming the children for the sins of the fathers has come to an end. The era of blaming the innocent for events beyond their control is on the wane, though not quite vanquished.

Today we are rethinking the very idea of what it means to honor thy father and mother. It no longer follows that loyalty is owed no matter what. We now point out that parents earn respect when they treat their children with love and respect. And we allow children to escape them, making their own destiny, if abuse has disguised itself as love. Today we recognize that becoming the hero of your own life means you might have to lose your family. For many people, healing begins with a deteriorating relationship with their parents, which might or might not be temporary. This is not only normal, it is a necessary stage of healing.

This is no Menendez solution, Jack, but the DNA needs to be liberated. How do you speak to a double helix? Through symbols and sound, vibrations that bypass intellect. This used to be done in societies as a matter of course. There were rituals that spoke directly to the unconscious, to the brain, to the cells themselves. These rites of passage employed a singular ordeal, group energy, symbolic images, rhythm, and voice to move the dependent youth toward dependable adult. But in our society we have elevated youth and eliminated rites of passage; we have forfeited the rituals that used to turn the switch in our brains, initiating us into our adult selves. The more we learn about the science of DNA, the less we understand how to speak to the soul of it. Let's face it, neither bar mitzvah nor confirmation cut the mustard. Graduation is just an all-night party. The images and sounds we consume produce anything but responsible individuality.

Without separation and initiation rituals, many of us are emotionally stunted in an eternal adolescence. Parents don't know how to follow through on their unique commitment to hand off the torch, instead simply abandoning their kids as they begin to threaten parental superiority. Adult children, like Oedipus, are emotionally, if not financially, dependent on the family legacy well into adulthood. Unlike Oedipus, many are afraid to detach from their parents' safety net and step out on their own path, no matter what the cost. Others remain stuck on the narrow bridge of rebellion, remaining attached to the battle for the road, but never winning it once and for all.

The tradition of a woman taking her husband's name in the ceremony of marriage dissolves her childhood identification with her father's authority. Unfortunately, it merely transfers her identity to another man's, rather than to herself. Plus, both women and men who change their names often feel the loss of an ancestry, one link that helps people feel connected to an enduring community. We need new rituals. We need to learn how to negotiate passage over that bridge. We may find new names or new meaning in our old ones.

Ritual Separation

I offer you such a ceremony to help you cross the bridge safely to your own psyche. Your folks won't die if you move on. After all, they have probably moved way beyond the place when those "tapes" of their voices got recorded in your brain. You might as well move on too, even if it feels like facing death. The following Practice Pages will show you how.

Don't get nervous. You can't do it wrong. And it blasphemes no one to structure your passage from the darkness into the light. Of course it won't go exactly as planned. I had not planned, for example, for the flock of finches who came to watch and sing to us from the grove during my ritual. Nor for the setting sun, which would disappear behind cloud cover as I named all the oppressive qualities I had internalized from my critical parents, begging to let them go. Nor either for the brilliant sunset that reached through as I affirmed my new hopes. Who knew that I would feel bottled up throughout the Native American, Celtic, and Hindu songs and chants that I had carefully chosen with my friends; that there would be no release during any of the heartfelt original prayers, nor the traditional Christian, Jewish, and pagan prayers that I said and heard. Obviously, I had wanted to cover every base, being attached to none in particular, but

I had not planned to feel nothing. I went through all the motions, following my script. I had enough faith in the power of healing ceremony to attribute my pent-up state to performance anxiety, knowing the results would still be true. Then the friend I had asked to spot me decided to improvise and did something unexpected. She took me in her arms and sang to me very quietly, just to me, an uncommon lullaby that I happened to know from long ago. Without warning, a shudder shook through me and the tears came down. Be sure to allow for the unexpected in your ceremony.

Among the many devotions I practiced to prepare for my ceremony, I made some representations of my parents, out of some garden-grown carrots that had sprouted double roots, making them two-legged. I wrapped them with embroidery floss, a different color for each personality trait that I remembered hurting me. My mother's sharp impatience, and my father's selfish small-mindedness, for example. The wrapping was an applied prayer, and in the praying I could feel how I had internalized almost every one of these qualities, becoming impatient and selfish myself. I recalled incidents where I had caused pain to others or myself in the same ways that made me so angry at my parents. During the ceremony, I listed the nasty traits, the humiliating incidents, the bad habits, like a litany, casting them out of me.

Then I set the dried carrots—my effigies of negative treasure—on fire, a symbolic act of alchemy, to transform the garbage to gold. The image of my mother's hurtful temper burned easily, as if the bad blood between us was old and dry tinder, long dead and short-lived, something we would outgrow. And that was borne out. But my father's would not burn. In fact it resisted all manner of annihilation, as if it were determined to maintain its power over me, becoming not a dummy to destroy but a fixed entity that held its energy. Finally I ripped it apart and buried it with the ashes of the other, not knowing what would grow in its stead. I knew by this that disgorging my innards of the muck between me and my father would take some doing. And so it has.

I said good-bye to my old self, held together with a temperament not entirely mine, and called for an open heart to let the real me emerge from this fresh place. I resolved to cut the strangling ties, leaving me only with the ample gifts they had each contributed to my being as well. And I gave birth to my new self, midwifed by my spiritual community, whose prayers for me would have brought tears to my own mother's eyes. I did not feel different immediately. It took some weeks. But when I did, the change in me was potent. I had changed my last name in the ceremony, and very quickly my new name stuck.

My family, especially the male members, was not terribly happy that I dropped their name. They felt rejected, I suppose. But it was not about rejecting them as much as it was about claiming myself as my own. The experience was a powerful bonding with my spirit, as well as a liberation of the family from my desire for them to change. Separation has cut both ways, inciting in all of us the freedom to regard one another as individuals.

Good-bye to All That

God may forgive you, but I never can.

—Elizabeth I, Queen of England
(to the Countess of Nottingham)

While you are practicing detachment, take care not to attach to the ideal of forgiveness. Consider that you can separate and move on without forgiving anyone but yourself. If you happen to come to it naturally, because people have changed or you have, it's a wonderful relief. It is especially appropriate when your dispute is over ways of being or thinking long since gone. If your actual parents no longer speak with the voices of that broken record playing in your head, then it's not about them anymore. It's about you. But I don't believe that healing and moving on requires forgiving perpetrators of abuse or evil, especially if they continue to abuse or do evil things.

By the same token, you do not need forgiveness from others to forgive yourself. Moving on is about accepting what happened, not absolving it. Absolution is not your job or anyone else's; it's God's. Healing is about forgiving yourself for having been small, weak, vulnerable, and even stupid. It may be that you have to release the argument or your insistence on being heard. That's part of what this descent into the dungeon is all about—letting go of any hope for others to change or need for your childhood to have been different. It wasn't. And they probably won't. Changing yourself is hard enough. Even laws are easier to change than people. You can organize against laws, but you can't organize against a lack of love. You can only teach yourself to find more of it elsewhere, to give it to yourself in the form of respect and care, and to give it to those who deserve it in your life today, especially your own children.

You will mourn. Moan and groan and grieve. You are supposed to cry about these things. And then you will look for all your reasons to live strewn among your belongings. You will find the food and water of life—the stuff that will resuscitate you—in the same bundles that starved and parched you. As you finish up your basement work and return to the surface, toward the airy reaches of adulthood that still seem nebulous and out of reach from this cavern, you can always retrieve what you shed, if you still want it. In addition, if you do not replace old habits with new ones, they will creep back into their familiar places. Pick up the discards that helped to ground you, cover you, and give you strength; some of these are the building blocks of your boundaries. You probably examined them while working the last chapter. Keep the stuff that gives your life substance. Leave behind what can't help you. Fill in with new bundles of hopes and dreams.

It doesn't work in a day. The good-byes are piecemeal, and each piece must be lamented. A friend's father used to tell her, "Cry some more, I'll give you a quarter." Her healing would finally begin when she cried every day for a year. We should be rich for all the crying. In fact, you avoid mourning at your peril. But cry at your own funeral, and you just may rise from the dead.

PRACTICE PAGES

Separation/Initiation Ceremony

Think of ceremony as an opportunity to refocus your energies and initiate your long-term plans. This process can take a day, a week, or months, depending on how much you want to put into it. You can call this a prayer circle or a theme party if that feels better than "ritual." It begins right now. Everything is praying.

1. **Enlist helpers.** Invite as many friends as you want, but at least one. Tell your supporters that you want their help to bury the dead past and initiate your potential future. Let each of them know why you want them there. Maybe because their input adds strength and power, maybe because you feel safe being born into the community they provide. You are in a sense asking them to be your new godparents. You might want to meet with them early to enlist their help with the preparations. You're going to make up an entire ceremony, so you may want some input from others you trust.

2. **Prepare yourself** and the circle for ceremony:

- Clean your basement, attic, garage, or storage area in the manner described in this chapter, as a working prayer. Discard at least one thing you don't need. Give away as much as you can. Your trash is another's treasure.

- Cleanse your mind by making a demonstration of prayers. I fashioned a circle out of 450 tobacco prayer ties wrapped around a talking stick. Maybe you'll want to make a quilt; each square is a prayer. Or repeat the Rosary for a moon's cycle.

- Fashion a sort of effigy, perhaps from a discard; the object should symbolize the *junk that is inside you,* which you would throw out if you could. Whether from your upbringing or elsewhere, this is internalized garbage. Plan for how you will dissolve its attachment to you. Fast if you'd like, but do it safely.

- Make or choose special giveaway items for everyone you have invited—things that represent those elements already in your life that you want to share. I have given and received everything from bread to art.

3. **Arrange separate areas and enough time** for the ritual and for the feast.

4. **Ask everyone to bring** an "altar" object (they can take it back afterwards) and a ritual activity to add to the mix:

   • A prayer, chant, song, poem, or story to help raise enough energy to separate you from what's wrong in your life—past or present—and to initiate your evolution from what's working for you now into your highest good.

   • A small symbolic giveaway item for you—a talisman of their hope for you or a symbol of their love.

   • Some food or beverage for the feast afterwards.

5. **Create the ceremonial area.** Make a circle of prayers, including a special place for the altar items that people will bring. Include anything special to your sense of the Creative Spirit. Candles and incense are used by almost every religious tradition on the planet. Don't limit yourself. Designate who will hold the "Power" places on the circle, those places that represent the world, the creator, the past, the future, body, mind, spirit, north, south, east, west, center, the altar; it's up to you. What are your Power places?

6. **Take a preparatory bath** in your home "temple" just prior to the Prayer Circle.

7. **Greet everyone** when they arrive in a friendly but formal manner. Treat this like the special event that it is. Get help to host the occasion if you want. You may have enough to do just taking care of yourself.

8. **Cast and close the circle** (like closing a game to additional arrivals) when everyone has settled and you are ready to begin. You can do this by any traditional or made-up method: holding hands, "smudging" with the smoke of sage, cedar, or incense, ringing a bell, etc. This begins the ritual, just as every religious service begins when all the participants have found their places in the hallowed hall.

9. **Call in the energies.** Go around the circle and call in the Spirit/s of All That Is in any way that feels comfortable, giving each person a chance to put their voice in the room in a sacred way. Just as the singers, cantor or cleric put their voices into the room to begin a service, invoke the energies of the Sacred Supreme. Build it up. Sing.

10. **State your case** to this Great Mystery. Say it, sing it, or chant it, but be specific and exhaustive. Go around the circle. Give everyone a turn. Let the energy get high and hot. Be sure to ask for

help in separating from what you don't want in your life at this time, and name the qualities of life you are seeking to increase. If you are using a medicine wheel format, go around the circle four times, describing what you are getting rid of and what you need. The first round is for your self—it's personal. The second is for family, the third community, and the fourth the world. *The idea is to move the energy first into the self and from there out to others.*

11. **Make a demonstration of separation.** For example, cut a cord that shackles you to the dungeon; destroy—shred, burn, melt, or bury—symbols of old ways of being bound; visualize sending unwanted attributes "out the door"; ceremonially pass them on to someone else who can use them productively or throw them out for you. Let go. Let yourself feel the loss. This is a kind of death; the end of the old you. Name the things you have accomplished, the things you've left undone, and the loved ones you leave behind. Say your good-byes. Cry for a vision.

12. **Receive the energy**. Open yourself to the changes taking place. Allow yourself the space to receive new energy through silence and stillness, or lamentation and keening. Let your circle hold the energy while you experience it flowing in and around you. Let them sing your praises, let them eulogize the old you who was well loved.

13. **Initiation.** When you can visualize yourself in the new life you desire, open your eyes! Rejoin the living. Behold, you are who you are. And be welcomed into your new sense of self like a little baby full of all the potential in the world. Listen as you are greeted by name. Go around the circle again, while each person expresses their hopes for you and gifts you with a symbol of those hopes. Listen with an open heart. Give thanks for your dreams coming true.

14. **Grounding the intentions.** Ritual in every tradition involves fixing the prayers into the body with food. Pass out your giveaways to the others in the ritual. Follow that with ritual food. This is akin to the Christian tradition of communion. Native Americans pass small amounts of traditional sacred food during the ceremony. Hindus and Buddhists finish meditation and blessing ceremonies with *prasad*, a taste of something sweet. The Shabbas meal begins the Jewish Sabbath, which is also ended with a meal twenty-four hours later.

15. **Clear the ritual space, to open the circle.** Affirm that everything you need to thrive exists on the planet and is available to you now. Give thanks to those Great Powers of Many Names who

have heard your needs and are preparing to meet them. Choose your Ideal Parents from these to call upon in the future. Many people are starting to embrace the idea of a Mother/Father God to embody this ideal figure. Tidy up any loose ends of energy with sound. This is the applause, the bell, the gong, or the amen that ends any ritual/performance. Connect by touch, voice, or eye contact with each and every person attending.

16. **Eat, dance, and celebrate.** This would be your post-ceremonial feast, your luau, your Sunday dinner. Earthly pleasures and worldly activities make the ritual *real.*

Within the next forty-eight hours, write about your experience and what you wish your life to look like from here on out, in the near future and in the distant future. Spend some special time in solitude over the next few weeks, allowing yourself to observe the transformation that is occurring within you as you detach from the past and attach to the possibilities that expand before you. Allow yourself to dream as you emerge from the Underworld back to the Light. Be ever mindful of the old ways you need to preserve, and those that are ready to fall away. Affirm your new program verbally, in writing, or in some other significant way. Welcome, the world is blessed to have you.

CHAPTER 8

SEX AND DREAMS: THE SANCTUARY

Just the word conjures up all kinds of lusty thoughts in adults: *Bedroom*. You know it when bringing a stranger in—say, a repairperson or inspector of some sort. You start the dance of poker faces, each of you jockeying to ignore the intimate nature of the room with its big loud BED standing open-armed in the middle and the closed drawers promising their intimate apparel hidden inside (or, God forbid, spilling out of them). It says way too much about you, you think. If there is only one bedroom in your home, it announces you as single and living alone, or sleeping with that other name on the mailbox; your sex life imagined while you stand there. And if there are two adult bedrooms, the absence of a regular sex life is assumed; you are pitied, sized up as pathetic. You're embarrassed. After all, no one really wants some subcontractor thinking about their bedroom life.

Not so with children. For them, "Come into my room," means you are gladly received into their private club, a place where grown-up rules are suspended and the spirit of the whole self-in-progress reigns. It's a special place—safe, scary, or both, depending on time of day, last movie seen, and overall confidence in the benevolent authority of the familiar adults. Kids who are lucky enough to have their own room are royalty among their peers, possessing the luxury of privacy and the power to enjoy it. On the other hand, sharing a room creates a lifelong bond—for good or ill—with a sibling.

To make this room a sacred space today is to integrate the child's view into the adult's, exalting both functions of the room—*sex and sanctuary*—with privacy and power. Add to that an understanding of the *holy order of sleep* and you face the trinity of rejuvenation in mind, body, and soul that this room supports. You could say the bedroom sleeps your sacred society, the inner circle where secrets are kept and shared only with the closest collaborator/s on your life journey. Maybe you record these secrets in your journal, maybe they are unveiled in dreams, maybe you share them with your partner, and maybe the communication is nonverbal.

I have known people who completely avoided the bedroom. They slept—*if* they slept—on the living room sofa in front of the unceasing TV. Their beds were used as catchalls for clothes, books, hobbies. It's common for children to avoid bedtime; but for these adults, it is more than not wanting to miss out on the fun. This is estrangement from soul, a feeling of betrayal in one direction or the other. A similar story is played out by the many who do go to bed, but keep the television on, fearing the quiet voice within. Some use timers that switch it off well after sleep has overtaken them, while others let it run all night long.

Then there are those who can't bear to leave the bedroom at all, using it as office, dining room, and family room. These cave dwellers live in the dark. Maybe they're artists, yearning for the proverbial garret. Maybe they're depressed. Maybe they haven't released their childhood soul into the rest of the house, or maybe they're keeping close tabs on the tether between body and soul. This is the room, whether in solitude, sleep, or sexual activity, where the mind passes through the realities of the body and beyond it into those states of consciousness traditionally linked with transformation.

You may have one of these shadow relationships with the bedroom if you were abused there. It is another sad fact that molestation, violence, and rape too frequently occur in one's own bed. In these circumstances, you begin to see how one can cut off from these sources of rest and renewal. But let's face it, serenity is not a given for any sanctuary. The first thing that such penetrating quiet brings is awareness of your own pain. And that's what scares us, isn't it? Who wants to feel that? Problem is, you have to "feel it to heal it."

Cleaning this room need not be a chore when you see the space as an inner sanctum for your daily resurrection. When you clean it that way, the room itself changes. And then you do, too. Issues of body image, sexuality, bad dreams, and sleep problems can complicate your experience of this room and we're going to get into them, since everyone struggles with these things on occasion.

Alone, Not Lonely: Solitude

Solitude renews your relationship with yourself. If you are feeling at cross purposes with your life or yourself, you need to improve the quality of your alone time, and actually connect with yourself. You do that by spending time alone in a sacred way.

There are many ways to spend this time. Julia Cameron writes in *The Artist's Way* about "artist dates" where you take yourself on outings that feed the creative spirit in you. I suggest you take her up on that, making yourself a friend who really understands: *you*. But if time is a problem, you can take a few minutes and do this at home, in your bedroom. If you are lucky enough to have other rooms where you spend creative time alone—an office, a sewing room, a studio, the garage, a home gym—then you are already engaging in some of this conversation with self. But if you are only using those rooms in their productive function, then you may need to make an adjustment to allow for receiving. In the bedroom, you have permission to be self-absorbed. In this place, you *need* to be interested in who you are.

The most basic time people spend with themselves is reading and writing. Not just any kind of reading and writing, but reading that takes you on an interior journey and writing that expresses it. Michael Silverblatt of NPR's *Bookworm* points out that this is the job literary novels once had, but is more and more frequently being given over to self-help books. In harried times like these, I guess, we need something that cuts to the chase. Still, there is nothing like a good novel to connect you with your own heart and the universal soul. Paradoxically, it's a TV personality, Oprah Winfrey, who is helping people get back to reading both kinds of books through her eponymous Book Club.

Whatever you've found, novel or nonfiction, spend some time reading a lengthy work before bed. It can be "mindless" like a mystery or a romance, but please not a magazine, a technical manual, or a professional journal. These tend to keep you out of your self and in your job or another social function. That's not a bedroom activity. Okay, well some magazines might be . . . but we'll save that for later.

People used to make art to call upon the sacred in the self. The tradition of singing or chanting along with it helped facilitate the journey. Sitting alone, or even quietly in a group, carving, sculpting, painting, sewing, weaving, quilting, etc., is often the best way to take you to the interior place of connection. I am convinced that women who cut out coupons on their bed while watching television are searching for this place but don't know how. Tell you what, after you've done your coupons, try making a collage. Cut out pictures that represent who you are deep inside. Or who you once were, or dream of yet becoming. Glue them on a sheet of poster board and hang it in your bedroom. Rekindle your sacred spark.

"Dear Diary" is a young girl's intuitive phrase to start the reach for her self in the Matmos, that "out there" place in the movie Barbarella where creativity begins. I know a grown-up writer who addresses her journal, "Dear Alfie," as in "What's it all about, . . . ?" It's often easier to remember to connect with a proverbial Other than with the self inside. But it's so essential to getting to that creative spirit that Julia Cameron instructs her readers to write three pages first thing each morning. Whether you write personal notes, morning or night, a story of your people, last night's dreams, or sketch out tonight's, let your bedroom remind you to take time to regularly correspond with the silent parts of yourself.

Keep the notebook by your bed if your family respects your privacy, in your underwear drawer if they need help with that. If your privacy is not respected at all by the people who share your life, then my guess is your solitude is a sad refuge full of secrets and fear. That's why we did boundaries and separating before we got to this chapter. Keep working on your vision of the ideal setting for your self and soul. You'll get there if you keep your "eyes on the prize." There is nothing more crucial to finding the sacred in your life than getting comfortable with solitude.

To Sleep, . . .

The most independent creature on the planet, the domestic cat, gets about eighteen hours of sleep a day. We adults in the free world can't seem to get the requisite eight. Some brag they're getting by on four, but that's nothing to brag about in my book. Without sleep, you're not dreaming. Without dreams, your heart drains out. Sleep is the place where you stretch the center of your energy field. It's been said we use only 10 percent of our brains. By that they mean 90 percent is unconscious. They say it to shame us, but it is so impervious to change that I'm beginning to believe it's supposed to be that way. If I'm right, then that explains why it's so important to spend a significant amount of concentrated time asleep and inanimate. And it's not supposed to be when you're awake.

Sleep renews all the systems of the body, including the ones that affect your psychological health. There is no place where the unity of the body and the mind is so clear as it is with sleep. Terrorists and tyrants know one of the most effective tortures is sleep deprivation, which makes you sick and psychotic. It not only undermines your physical fitness, it impairs your judgment, eventually making your very reality suspect. No matter how high your pain threshold, when you lose understanding of your perceptions, you lose the ability to make clear choices. While most of us will never be tortured this way, thank goodness, many people are asleep in their lives and awake in bed. Maybe there's a connection there. Respect and exalt your sleep time. The ancients knew it was sacred time, but our lust for success rather than soul has made us forget at our peril.

Insomnia and other sleep problems are pandemic. As with all health concerns, if you have a sleep disorder, you should first consult your health practitioner to ensure it is not physiological. You may need treatment. The second thing to check is home security. Often sleeplessness is related to feelings of powerlessness and fear of violation. This is how your own self tortures you. Go ahead and take the practical measures to make your home as safe as possible for sleeping. A sense of security is a palpable thing—just ask anyone who doesn't have one. Create an environment of safety like any good parent handling the sleeplessness and scary dreams common to children. That's the least you can do for yourself.

To create a feeling of security, you need a multi-dimensional approach: physical, emotional, and metaphysical. For kids, that might mean that one parent checks under the bed, in the closets, and in the drawers, while the child looks on. Or a parent might read a story about another kid surviving a wild night, such as Maurice Sendak's *In the Night Kitchen* or Robert Louis Stevenson's epic poem "Winken, Blinken, and Nod." A hall light or a special night-light may be left on. In loving families, a child troubled in sleep has permission to call out or crawl into bed with Mom and Dad, waking them up and telling their terrors. Figure out the equivalent for yourself. In my house, it's as likely to be J. K. Rowling's Harry Potter books as anything, and none of the kids here are under forty.

Lakota Sioux medicine man and psychologist Phil Lane tells a story of a group of convicted felons with whom he was working using traditional sacred ceremonies. As I remember it, the prisoners in one sweat lodge ceremony heard him pray for his eight-year-old son, who had been suffering from nightmares since he and his wife had recently separated. Each of those men knew all too well what it was to be afraid in the night. The next week they gave Phil a protective talisman for his son, a medicine necklace made in the style of a Navaho squash blossom design. Usually crafted in turquoise and silver, this one was made of blank rifle shells donated by the prison's guards. Each man prayed over it, imbuing it with his own personal vow to protect his spiritual leader's youngster in the dreamtime, where he would learn to be a strong and loving man. The little boy hung it by his bed and his nightmares ceased. Just like that. He had the toughest men in imagination on his side against the night's demons.

Some of these methods will work for you as well. After all, it's the child in you that can't handle the grown-up anxieties that are keeping you awake. The following suggestions fall into four categories of attack: prevention; repairs and remedies; aid and comfort; and metaphysics.

Insomnia Prevention

- Avoid scary or upsetting movies before bed; don't watch the eleven o'clock news.

- Avoid caffeine, if not entirely, at least three hours before bedtime. Avoid food three hours before bedtime.

- Dim the lights a couple of hours before bedtime to slow down your internal clock.

- Block out sounds with a white noise machine or air cleaner that will block the house's creaks and groans.

- Block out light with blackout curtains and a draft tube under the door.

Repairs and Remedies

Most police departments and insurance companies will send a security specialist to your home free of charge to help you beef up your home security. They may recommend some of the following:

- Motion-sensitive security lights that will illuminate the dark places in your yard or house if someone walks by.

- Good locks, extra locks, and locked and wired windows.

- Alarm systems (inexpensive ones are available at stores like Radio Shack).

- Organized security like a security company or volunteer Neighborhood Watch group.

Besides prescription and over-the-counter sleeping medications, there are alternative, traditional, and natural remedies such as:

- Beverages: hot milk with vanilla; chamomile tea.

- Herbs and supplements: valerian, kava kava, melatonin, and premixed combinations thereof.

- Homeopathic: Rescue Remedy.

Aid and Comfort

- Take a well-established self-defense course that utilizes full-force fighting, issue-oriented counseling, and bedroom scenarios such as those taught by Impact Personal Safety/Prepare, Inc.

- Use the support people you've listed on your Personal Elementary Alternative Resource List (PEARL) from chapter 5. Emotional safety comes from having people you can call if you are scared. You may not be able to crawl into bed and tell Mommy your bad dreams, but maybe you have someone who will listen to them and help you deconstruct them. Write them in a dream journal if you don't.

- Masturbate! It releases pent-up energy like a steam valve. A good vibrator will minimize any exertion required. Good Vibrations out of San Francisco offers them by mail order.

Metaphysics

But how do you intervene in nightmares about intangible enemies? You probably don't have your own group of tough guys who will fashion a personal talisman, but don't underestimate the power of metaphysics to bolster your feeling of well-being.

- Make your own protective talisman and hang it in a "power place" in your bedroom.

- Do some journal work dialoguing with your "inner child-self," assuring your unconscious that there is nothing in the nonmaterial world that can't be handled.

- Practice heroic dream scenarios to equip yourself with defensive strategies to take into your unconscious for "lucid dreaming." Lucid dreaming is a technique to increase conscious awareness of dreaming *while* dreaming. The goal is to learn to use the nonlinear, nonphysical reality of dreams to your own advantage, changing the dream scenario for power or peace. Tell yourself to know you are dreaming if you are in an absurdly violent scenario. Remind yourself that laws of physics and logic don't exist in dreams; proceed from there to *win*.

- Set a clear intention to be protected from spiritual battles in your sleep by the use of a "Gatekeeper" (the practice pages at the end of this chapter will guide you). Ask that all "lessons" come gently and sweetly, and make good on your commitment to learn from them by recording *all* dreams, not just the bad ones.

- Fashion or request a "Dream Walker"—a personal Hero who will join you in your dreams and help you fight and conquer your own night demons (*Dreamscape* 1984).

- *Remember: you have the Universal Right to survive.* Practice getting and setting clear priorities and boundaries in your mind and in your dreams. Dreams are a good way to practice fighting for your life *by any means necessary.*

- Most importantly for insomniacs, though, the trick is to find your quiet inner self. For me, it's making all those righteous speeches when I'm trying to go to sleep that sends me to the Tylenol PM. Try to think of this awake time as quality time with that self. Commune with your daydreams, connecting spirit with Spirit.

- Practice a meditation technique that utilizes a *mantra*, such as Transcendental Meditation or Womoncraft. It helps to quiet the mind's uncontrolled thoughts, which are often the cause of insomnia. Until you've learned a technique, you can use any soft-sounding single syllable. For example, count backwards slowly from TEN to ONE on your exhale. Then repeat the number *ONE* over and over as your mantra. Hold a symbolic image of that number in your mind's eye at the same time until your breathing grows deep and you fall asleep. *Program* your mind to know that the sound of *ONE* along with the picture of *ONE* relaxes the mind, emptying it. Every time a stray thought interrupts the repetition of the word, simply notice it and let it go, reestablishing your focus on the mantra. You might combine this method with a visualization of a "safe place" or a paradise where all your needs are met without effort.

- Or, do about twenty-five sit-ups to exhaust the churning energy in your third chakra, the seat of mental activity (Bruyere 1989). Now try meditating again. Go on a journey underground to meet your shadow teacher and ask for comfort and self-acceptance. As long as you're awake, you may as well have a deep heart-to-heart with your small, quiet inner voice. If you really listen and habituate that kind of relationship, your insomnia will become scarce. If it doesn't, go back to the doctor and look again for a medical cause.

- One last, radical tactic. Stay up. Maybe your "muse" is calling. Creative energy can keep you awake, changing your sleep cycle—ask any artist, musician, or writer. As I write this, it is 3:45 A.M. This is not insomnia; this is "flow." When the world is asleep and the dreamers are flying about, creative energy is readily available. Find the form that wants to express itself through you and explore the night!

... Perchance to Dream ...

Dreams are the movies that renew your psyche. You're the protagonist in these shows, grappling with your own human condition. Dreams give your fears a place to unravel. They give your guilt a place to confess, your grief a place to unload, your desire and your taboos a place to play together. The good thing is that you are not even remotely responsible for them. Jealous mates and guilty consciences need to get clear on that. Whereas the mind and the body are accountable for the choices we make, and are bound by the ideals we choose to follow, dreams belong to your heart and your soul, and they march to a different drummer. Protect them as you would freedom of speech. Censorship has no place in the absolute democracy of your brain.

Dreams belong to the gods themselves. They mix genres, combining steamy sex with comic absurdity, thrilling suspense with slasher gore, cartoon violence with foul matter. Whether they are scary, sexy or silly, black or blue, dreams are free as creation.

That doesn't mean they aren't disturbing. I had a whole barrage of recurring sex dreams during the period of my life when I regarded everything except genuine and meaningful communication as *unclean*. Wild frenzied sex, mostly with unabashed pop icons. I was appalled. And thrilled.

Lots of people have sexual dreams about celebrities. I wonder if it taxes the celebrities' psyches; if they feel invaded, being stalked even in the astral. Sex dreams deal with the psyche's *urge to merge*, either willingly or unwillingly, with certain qualities. For instance, a superstar's ego, their popularity, their work ethic. Or their talent, their wealth, their beauty and power. Dreams like these can help you make a commitment to work on the qualities you want to internalize or to investigate. Personally, I was sorely in need of some ideological freedom.

More upsetting are rape dreams, which may connote attachments that are painful or unwanted. Such dreams are not wish fulfillment, as psychoanalysts once suggested, nor are they actual memories, as some recovery zealots might claim. However, they might illuminate denied dynamics in a relationship or a situation, such as core violation.

This is not to say that a dream of any sort can't derive from a memory, conscious or hidden. It very well might. But dreams tend to be representative or symbolic, not literal or expositional. If you can hang in there, despite your reaction to the nightmare of them, they can show you where you need boundaries or help you to know when to detach from people, places or things; when to communicate more effectively with them; and when you need to do some more in-depth exploration of your life.

As disconcerting as they are, nightmares are a true godsend. They are your unconscious mind saying to you: *Okay, I've tried to show you in gentle, subtle terms and you just won't get it, you forget your dreams, argue with your inner guidance, ignore the angels . . . try ignoring this . . .* And WHAM! You get a vivid, knock your eyes open, cold sweat Wes Craven of a dream—something you can't forget. Give yourself an Oscar; you now have some great material for your therapist. Respect your nightmares. They are as surely gifts from the Divine as a spiritual trance is to an oracle. Scary, yes. But not lethal. In occasional doses, they are good medicine.

In fact, killing your dream enemies develops your commitment to survival. If you can take a risk safely anywhere, it's in your dreams, where your real body is safe in your bed. This is the place to practice facing your greatest fears, by fighting the monsters in your dream world. You won't actually hurt anyone—there is nothing permanent about the dreamscape. Everything comes back. My grandfather has been dead twenty-five years, but he still shows up to take me to his favorite restaurant in my dreams. Of course, returning enemies are less welcome. The dream world is like a jungle, and the rules are the same. If you find yourself in a nightmare, be prepared to kill or be killed. Use whatever metaphysical tools you can amass: holy helpers, power animals, medicine objects, and visualization. This is where they work.

Naked dreams, flying dreams, toilet dreams, mute dreams, slow-motion dreams, heroic dreams, victim dreams—if you describe any dream in colloquial language, your own words may explain it to you: overexposed, free flying, pissed off and full of shit, mute, slow to move, stuck, you're great, you're a victim. When you write down your dreams, be sure to read them out loud so you can hear the symbolism beneath the words that you choose to describe them. Don't forget to listen to the brutally honest language of your dreams. "My shit was all over the place" says a lot more to you than "there was feces on the floor."

. . . Ah, There's the Rub . . .

Sex is the phoenix rising from the flames. It's also the snake in the grass, coiled and ready to strike. The French call an orgasm *le petite mort*, literally "little death." The sign of Scorpio governs both sex and death because they are believed to transform the soul in related ways, giving you another chance. Sex takes you to the brink and resurrects you. It literally stimulates your life force. No wonder it's procreative.

Then why do so many people admit to sexual dysfunction? What does that mean anyway? Maybe they just don't like their partners, or the way their partners make love to them. This is a dance, folks—no one wants their toes crushed in bed. Pay attention to what you're doing. Take a shower. Trim your nails. You are meeting with Creation.

You've heard the joke: *Bad sex is like bad pizza—even when it's bad, it's still pretty good.* What I want to know is, who laughs at this joke? I mean besides sex addicts and junk food junkies? Bad sex to me is like bad shellfish. It makes me want to retch. The fact is, there are a zillion books on how to improve a failing sex life, entire professions dedicated to repairing sexual dysfunction. This must mean that, for lots of people, sex is a nightmare.

It's not surprising. After all, we have a sexually perverted culture. We use a corrupted form of sex to sell consumer products. We link sex with violence to sell movies, and to rate them. Yet if news gets out to the religion police that someone enjoys it outside its reproductive context, they are engulfed in scandal and shame. No wonder people carry baggage with their sexuality. You're no good unless you're sexy; if you're sexy you're no good. Additionally, if, like one in four girls or one in seven boys, you were introduced to an adult's sexuality inappropriately as a child, your baggage includes having your own developmental process violated, shamed, and possibly brutalized. Sexual abuse wounds the very soul, separating you from your instinctual sanctuary.

But let's face it, sex would be rife with hazard in the best of circumstances—it's about people getting naked with all their issues of trust, boundaries, power, and performance just hanging out. So to speak. Sex is not easy for anyone. This is not a bad thing. Sex is *supposed* to be down and dark and hot and heavy. Even when you and your partner know your way around the dance floor pretty darn well—pure, easy, and smooth—sex is grunting and groaning and earthy, it's heavy breathing, it's undignified, it's *fecund.*

Approach this most transformational of all activities mindfully, as you do living in the rest of your house. Especially with curiosity and indulgence for taboo feelings and suppressed images, even if you find out you hate what you're supposed to like, and like what you're supposed to hate. Let this be a lifelong pursuit, because that's intimacy for you. If sex has gotten dull and boring with a longtime partner, my guess is you have long since stopped that mindful pursuit. Try approaching one another as beloved strangers. Maybe you don't know everything there is to know about one another. Have you ever kissed their elbows?

What is the point of looking at sex from a sacred point of view? Does it help us as human beings to be able to express these taboos and suppressed images? Yes, especially if you are using taboo as an excuse to limit your relationship with your soul, or suppressing images to prevent yourself from healing the injuries that put them there. This is not to say you have to engage in taboo activity. In order to be soulfully sane you have to let your mind be free and open, even if you are choosing to limit your sexual behavior. On the other hand, if you find yourself expressing the *shadow* of your psyche through sexual behavior, there is probably something for you to learn there. Find out what it is.

The Episcopal cleric John Alexis Viereck points out that Jung spoke about the "shadow" as "those aspects of ourselves that do not fit in with our self-image or the values of our family and culture" (1988, 2). You will find them in yourself in those parts you have "repressed, denied, disowned and/or projected onto others and perceived as bad or [threatening]." That doesn't mean they are. Nor does it mean that they're not.

Sexual thoughts, fantasies, dreams, and behaviors are particularly affected because they are so hard to control. In fact, these impulses are neither bad nor good, but when they are unconscious we tend to experience them as an attack on our very serenity. If we continue to disown them, however, they can become our undoing. Initial critical judgment of your own shadow will likely cause you to disown your sexuality, when what you need to do is become aware of it, recognizing it as part of you. Jungian therapists Connie Zweig and Steve Wolf (1997) call this work "romancing the shadow." It is the only way I know of to free our sexuality to its sanctuary potential. These are some of the things you will find in the shadow of your bedroom:

Fantasies You Hate to Have

It's a well-kept secret. Many women have fantasies of being bound, dominated, and raped by men and groups of men, including teenagers and father figures. They also imagine dominating and disciplining men into giving them pleasure. This doesn't mean the average woman wants the chance to experience any of these brutalities in real life. On the contrary, taking charge of the fantasy can create a situation of dominating the dominator; allowing a "safe"—i.e. *imaginary* and controlled—scenario for submission. But it is important to realize that the prevalence of these fantasies in Western women is an indication of the misogynistic and self-destructive images still lurking in the darkness of our culture and consciousness.

Less secret are the male fantasies about controlling women sexually and raping them. Some men even get turned on by thoughts of killing and dismembering women. But men also imagine scenes of being dominated by older women like their mothers, or punished by their sisters. These too are expressions of the shadow. The problem, again, is that such fantasies also reveal the underside of the patriarchal culture that has a real history of torturing women sexually. Irresponsible individual behavior can come of it. When we are unaware of the "shadow that lurks in the hearts of men," it becomes "an abandoned and exposed space through which evil can work" (Viereck 1988, 2).

On this I am unequivocal: torture, brutality, enslavement, and related persecutions for any reason, including but not limited to sexual pleasure, are evil. But is thinking, fantasizing, or role-playing them evil? Perhaps these shadowy thoughts let us know what we are capable of as a human race. Perhaps knowing what we are capable of keeps us honest, if not always honorable, healthy if not perfected.

Another secret that may shock some people: Incestuous and adult-child sexual response seeps into the feeling and fantasy life of "ordinary people," just as it does perpetrators of sexual crimes as well as survivors of such betrayal. If you are unaware of how natural and beautiful is this visceral "ache for purity," as one colleague of mine put it, this may be the most disturbing of responses to have. But the aberrant behavior of acting out such thoughts can only thrive when the thought lodges in a disowned place of your sexual being, where impulse control is the only guard. That is where it threatens to control behavior and get acted out into perpetrating conduct. By the same token, such imprisonment of thought can create so many rules for the person suffering from taboo feelings that they may prevent themselves from having any intimacies at all, replacing passion with a wholesale rejection of sexuality. Others may compulsively seek out unhealthy relationships.

Sex brings up so many questions about shame and taboos that one can only wonder how necessary they are to sexual desire. Might indulging in shameful taboo fantasies even be appropriate at times? For example, when we make love for the first time or with a new partner, don't we need to break down the social barriers to get there and even more to find the pleasures of the other? At other times, isn't there a difference between thinking something and doing it? Is "lusting in your heart," as President Jimmy Carter was vilified for admitting, a real sin? Is a thought bad simply because it does not fit your values or the values of your community? I don't think so. In fact, the possibility of both thinking and doing may be necessary to a passionately open mind. What if lust is more than thought? What if it's behavior? Whether or not it's wrong depends on whether someone is violated by the behavior. When does dipping into the darkness lead to immoral choices? What makes impulse control so easy for some and so difficult for others? When does acting out a taboo become evil?

These are important questions to explore, ones I can't answer for you. Opening up to your sexuality requires a willingness to ask the questions for yourself. Forming answers with a trusted partner will give your sexuality a safe framework for intimacy.

Inappropriate Attractions

You're a teacher and the fresh, mid-puberty adolescent sitting in the third row turns you on; you have a dream one night of having sex with her/him and wake up mortified. You are not a child molester, even a secret one—just as the teenager is not a seducer for dreaming of sex with you, the teacher. As a teenager you jerked off to your science teacher's picture in the yearbook. She was a nun. You still think of her sometimes when you're making love to your wife. Neither woman would be thrilled to know this. Or would they? You're attracted to your boss's spouse and have a three-way in dreamland. Well, now that's been a movie once or twice. You think of sex every time you have dinner with friends. Suddenly someone at the table starts berating people who think about sex at every odd moment; you try not to give yourself away.

While we are a sex-obsessed culture, there's also a major "no talk rule" about actual sex and sex thoughts. While sexually transmitted diseases (STD's) are at epidemic proportions for adults and teens alike, the only folks talking about sex are researchers who write books about the desperate people who ask for help or the kinky ones willing to be research subjects—a hybrid group, I'm sure. The great thing about the HBO television show *Sex and the City*, is that it is normalizing the wide variety of ways average women think about, fantasize about, talk about, have, and avoid having sex.

Let's go with the understanding that sex is weird. There is nothing else in daily life that even compares to getting naked with another person and probing pungent apertures. The fact that a particular form of it produces children is *irrelevant*. That detail, I'm convinced, is the Universe's way of keeping the terminally uptight from outlawing pleasure altogether. Beyond that, you could endlessly debate which are weirder: "natural" acts or "taboo" ones. As far as what is good and right and acceptable, it comes down to two measures: Is everyone involved capable of knowing whether it feels good to them, and are they each free to decline? That precludes adults from engaging in it with kids, other adults with disabilities that render them immobile or defenseless, and some subordinate relationships. That's it. The rest should be your choice.

S&M and Pornography: Some Like It Hot, Some Like It Not

Have you ever wanted someone so much you wished you could possess them or own them, and be owned by them? If you haven't, I am truly sorry. Desire can be so palpably powerful that the idea of tying someone up so they can't leave you can seem, on some level, practical, not kinky. The same can be said for accepting a lover's dominance over your very soul. The condition can feel precast. Some would ask, why *not* play it out with your bodies? Or at least watch it played out on screen. Such is the logic behind sadomasochism and pornography—for those of us searching for justification.

S&M pushes some serious buttons. Debates rage, dividing conservatives, middle of-the-roaders, libertarians, liberals, feminists, gays, and lesbians in a free-for-all. Right wing Christians are unanimously against it, that doesn't mean none engage in it. They just do it in secret. In addition, one might think that sex games of slavery would not be attractive to anyone who had been enslaved, that brutality would not be at all arousing to anyone who had been brutalized, that imbalanced power would not turn on anyone who had suffered with powerlessness. However, one would be wrong. Participants in sadomasochism as well as bondage and discipline (B&D) cross divisions of class, race, gender, sociohistorical, and sexual backgrounds. Again, to be clear, this type of sex turns me off ideologically. I don't buy the rationale. That doesn't mean I don't respond to the imagery, whether I want to or not.

However, my discomfort with pornography, S&M, and all the varieties of sex play that utilize objectification and pain comes down to one major point, and it's not ideological. It's because it does turn me on and I would rather it didn't. Why would I rather it didn't? Because to get turned on by images that bear striking resemblance to torture and slavery offends my very soul. It rubs me the wrong way. And frankly, the way you get rubbed ultimately determines whether you get off. There's a short circuit between turn on and takeoff. For me. But the fact that I am turned on in the first place shines a light on the stuff lurking in my shadow.

What can be retrieved from the passionate animal lust evident in S&M and missing from "married sex"? What are those charged images brightened by the black light and infrared of the darkened room? Remember that, at its best, sex renews life force.

Life force is the connection between *power* (over creation itself) and *responsibility* (taking care of what's created). It is desire that knows no limits. The pain of love. The mystery in the male body's readiness to mate. The miracle of the female body's ability to respond, facilitating wanted and unwanted penetration alike. Without endorsement or decision. Without equivocation. The intense lust to live. Survival stories entice us because of that feeling. And so does pornography. It shows our desperate need to feel alive.

For those adult survivors of sexual abuse who shake and sweat with guilt for having experienced sexual response from the abusive acts against their spirits and bodies, this is important information. *The body is designed to respond.* You couldn't help it when your body responded with the first assault. That's what it was designed for. It's reflexive, it's protective, it's out of anyone's conscious control. This reality is quite possibly the greatest attraction to rough sex: "Recreate the scenario and see for yourself." Isn't that part of the S&M agenda?

In a loving partnership, it's possible to find a safe way to explore these feelings of power and surrender, passion and desire, the lines where want crosses into rage, love into hate, good into evil. Finding sacred space in the bedroom is about awareness and *awakeness* in the darkness. It is not about making allegiances to the darkness. But it's also not about making rules and restrictions against taboo feelings. The prostitute-priestesses of ancient Egypt, Greece, and Celtic regions knew the potential in unfettered sexuality. Their sacred art transformed the fertile psyches of their devotees through desire and orgasm.

One thing I'm sure of: The freer you and your partner feel to explore a broad range of sexual feelings and ways of touching, giving and receiving pleasure, the deeper your intimacy and the better your sex. This can be hard if you have a heavy ideology about what is "correct" sexual behavior and response. It is also difficult if you have no idea what you think about sex either as an individual or as a couple. Compatibility is defined by the ongoing conversation of ideas and feelings between you and your partner, as well as physical chemistry and compatible "technique." You don't have to make it up; there are video tapes and CDs of people having sex all over the place. There are magazines showing it. The difference between pornography and erotica is "in the eye of the beholder," in my view. Then again, it can be a lot of fun to just make it up.

Cleaning the Sanctuary

Begin with hopelessness—if you begin with enthusiasm,
you fall on your face.

—James Hillman, *Inter Views*
(with Laura Pozzo)

Okay, so it's hopeless. Sanctuary, sleep, dreams. Sex. A nightmare quest for inner peace, the zipless fuck, the dreamless sleep, and now we're supposed to learn to dream *consciously*—with this lucid dreaming business? How can we hope for sanctuary under so much pressure? Still, we continue to seek asylum in the bedroom. And when we find it, ah . . . the refuge of sleep, the reverie of dreams and the resurrection of sex, bringing sweet relief to body, soul, and spirit.

Your task, then, is to prepare your room to use in retreat. Look closely at the subtext of a room where both withdrawal and encounter occur. Remember: The very nature of this room is renewal. The first thing you want to do in cleansing this room is to remove everything that is in the way of these renewals.

Because we drop and leave our dirty clothes here, because we toss and turn for several hours in sheets that stay on the bed for days if not weeks, it should come as no surprise that the bedroom is a magnet for dead skin cells, hair, dust, and lint—which we proceed to breathe in all night long. Can you say, "respiratory nightmare"? That's why it's a good idea to dust and vacuum frequently—even more than in the rest of the house, you know how to do it—followed by dust or damp mopping, especially under the bed. You'll sleep better.

If you use a Miele or other vacuum with a HEPA filter, you will not have to dustmop after vacuuming, because it emits almost 0% residual fine dust particles. In addition, especially if you have allergies, you should: clean vents and filters each time you vacuum; use blinds and shades instead of drapes and curtains; do not use a bed skirt (it's a dust collector); seal the door with weather stripping, especially at the bottom, to cut down on lint and dust drifting in while you sleep; use an air cleaner; and install a HEPA filter in your central air and heating system.

Clothes and Clutter

Keep a basket in the room to contain dirty clothes and use it instead of the floor. If you are in the habit of wearing things more than once that you can't put away with clean clothes, invest in a valet (*not* the man, the furniture piece) or at least a straight-backed chair. Tossed clothes do not interfere with the ambience of this room; the intimacy of them truly belongs here. But plan for them so they have a proper place to settle. As far as putting away and hanging up the clean ones . . . I refuse to nag. It's your room.

The Bed

Once you get the junk off the bed, make it. Lots of people hate to make their beds. I use Sundays as a holiday from making mine, but then getting into bed Sunday night is kind of a drag. That's the best reason for making the bed, because there's nothing like climbing into fresh sheets. If you wash your sheets on Sundays, you can still not make the bed and then get into soft and clean ones that night and really start your week out right. Heloise suggests putting them on the bed straight from the dryer and they'll "iron themselves." I would wonder who still irons sheets if my own partner hadn't wanted the new ones ironed "to break them in." Okay. I don't buy no-iron sheets and I don't iron them. Heloise and I are right in synch.

I like to make the bed before I even get out of it. Grab the top sheet, blankets, bedspread and all, in both fists, flap them out once to even them across the bed, and pull them up. Slide yourself out the top or the side, and boom, you're done. With the bed made, you're already well on your way to a proper refuge.

An important note: For a comfortable sleep, use untreated cotton sheets with at least a 200-thread count. Cotton is not a quality (as people with polyester sheets seem to think), it's a specific kind of fabric. It isn't a blend, it isn't percale. 100% cotton (or damask linen if you can afford that) is what your body wants to sleep in. Satin—the luxury imposter—does not breathe, and consequently your skin gets hot, you perspire in the night, and don't get the rest your body needs. Nothing but natural fiber sheets breathes properly for a sleeping body. If you have very sensitive skin, the higher the thread count, the better. True luxury is sleeping in well worn, unbleached, undyed Egyptian cotton with a thread count over 350. Yum.

There are no hard and fast rules on how to make a bed. Some people like their sheets tucked in all around, some only on the bottom end, and some need it all open. Some folks like lots of blankets, others only a comforter. Not everyone likes a bedspread; others think it is required. The great thing about a comforter is you can throw it over an unmade bed and voilá—it looks made. Make your bed the way *you* feel cozy in it.

Creature Comforts

Making the bedroom a sacred space involves having things in it that make you feel divine. Sacred is not a hair shirt and a straw pallet. Sorry, martyrs, but it just isn't. Sacred is everything you've ever heard it was: your body on a bed of clouds, your head on a pillow of air, the sweet scent of milk and honey, a vision of loveliness, the voices of angels, and the gasp of inspiration. Deprivation does not make you feel worthy of heaven and earth; it makes you feel like dirt, living in hell. If your alone time, your sleep, and your lovemaking are going to be worthy of Creation itself, get all your bedroom needs met. It's your sanctuary.

You're going to want to read and write in here. You might want a vibrator, safe sex products, *toys* even, ear plugs, hand cream, manicure tools, candles, in addition to the requisite lamp, clock radio, and a telephone for security (with ringers you can turn *off*). Make a place for the materials you want to have. It doesn't have to be a gorgeously expensive bedroom suite; it does have to be handy for you. Convenient. As if you were being served by angels.

It's typical to have reading matter stacked by the bed. A shelf or cabinet is better of course, mostly because it's easier to keep clean. Truly, I have not seen a perfect solution for this dilemma. Bookshelf headboards are uncomfortable to lean against. Side tables without drawers get cluttered too fast; those with drawers have accessibility problems. I have always had a stack of books, magazines, newspapers, and letters next to my bed that I cannot organize with any satisfaction. So much for good intentions.

Pulling It Together

If you're having difficulty making this room feel like a sanctuary, it may be time to bring in a feng shui practitioner. Pronounced "fung shway," it's the ancient Chinese art of placement. Literally meaning "wind and water," feng shui aims to create harmony inside living spaces with the forces of nature. It offers a whole host of suggestions for arranging your bedroom for optimal energy flow. According to this art, the bedroom is the most important room in the house in terms of establishing harmonious energies for health, wealth, and balance for individuals, relationships, families, and communities (Finster 1991).

Feng shui problems may be the most noticeable in the bedroom because sleep, sex, and feeling safe are all about the energy of a room. How does the energy flow in your bedroom? Forthwith, the Westernized economy version: The energy should come in through the door and circle the bed. Arrange dressers and accessories to that effect. Furthermore, the head of the bed should not be beneath a window, nor the foot of it facing the door. Good luck.

This is a gross generalization, but as such, true enough—pictures and artwork in the public parts of the house, like the living room, serve the celebration or stimulation of your social being: family life, entertainment, discourse, and the like. But in the bedroom, the inspiration provided by décor—color, texture, mood, image—should be primarily for your enjoyment. This isn't a guest room, or a hotel room; therefore it need not be decorated like one. It should be personal. Here are a few ideas about how to make it your own:

- What will give your eyes refuge when you look around this room? What hues, textures, and ideas do you want to surround you in sanctuary? Maybe waterscapes, portraits, or sketches inspire you to dream. Perhaps rosewood, chenille, or muslin soothes your eyes as well as your naked skin. Restful colors might be greens, peaches, eggshell, or midnight blue. Offer the first level of rest to your senses.

- Maybe you want your erotic life expressed here. Depictions of lovers or nudity—whether or not the works are originals, reproductions, or simply snapshots—are not inappropriately provocative in your private boudoir.

- Maybe you want your emotional life reflected. Pictures of people you love, who make you happy to see them, are common. Homemade pasteboard collages of your healing process can be put on these walls to remind your unconscious of the work you are doing. If photos of your family make you twitch (especially during sexual activity) even though you love them, display them in the foyer, instead of the bedroom. If they provide the most warmth in your life, by all means gather them around you in your retreat.

- A mirror is nice, not only for dressing, but also for the light it adds to the room both in terms of illusion and illumination. It keeps the energy (in this case as light) moving. According to feng shui, a hanging mirror placed properly can enhance a room in indescribable ways, "like a brilliant schooner does a harbor" (Finster 1991). It enlivens the room and increases personal energy (ch'i) while deflecting the unwanted effects of external energies (i.e., other people). It offers a view of hidden parts of the room. In Western terms, it gives the illusion of lifting the ceiling and enlarging the room. Some people shudder at the sight of a mirror. If that's you, put it behind the closet door. But if you can stand it, a mirror offers the room a doorway into a sort of magic, like water in an oasis.

A Final Note for Sensitive Sleepers

If you have allergies, controlling the dust, lint, and feathers in the bedroom means being able to breathe through the night. Other sensitivities to noise, light, textures, and crowding are no less important to your ability to receive the blessing of sleep.

- **Allergies:** Cover feather pillows with plastic or cloth, zippered pillow covers, one of each even, and a cotton pillowcase over those. Cover feather comforters as well, or better yet, use a fiberfill one. Most pillows—even feather pillows—can be washed in the washing machine, which will keep them fluffed and dust mite free. To dry them faster, place a clean tennis shoe or tennis ball in the dryer with them.

- **Noise:** Mask it with a white noise machine, air cleaner, fan, or air conditioning. Hang heavy drapes or rugs to simulate soundproofing (if you are allergic to drapes, vacuum them often or raise the volume of your white noise instead). Use soft foam earplugs— they're comfortable and keep out noise levels so intense that airport runway professionals use them.

- **Light:** If blackout curtains are not doing the trick, keep a *soft*, black eye mask nearby for optional use. If it's still too light, cover the windowpanes with dark paper.

- **Texture:** If the proverbial princess and the pea have nothing on you, then you feel bumps, crumbs, even hairs and threads that no one else can even *see*. Try flipping your mattress, letting the dents fall out. Stay away from sheets made of polyester blends that tend to "pill." 100% *untreated* cotton may wrinkle, but it will not get nubbly as it wears. Rather, it will get softer and smoother. Get yourself a soft nylon dust brush or a lint roller and use them *only* for sweeping out the sheets before you get in them at night. Make your bed religiously to keep the day's dust from settling between the exposed covers.

- **Space:** If you are claustrophobic, the way the bed is made may feel like a matter of life and death to you. You may feel "allergic" to sharing sheets, or even to sharing a bed at all. Don't despair, you are not alone. And there are ways around your idiosyncrasies, whether or not you are working to "normalize" them. If you need separate beds from your partner, you need separate beds. You don't have to give up the partner. Or you can get a larger bed: the larger the bed, the easier it is to share. You don't need to be a large man to need a king-size bed. If you are a small woman with big needs, think seriously about spending the money on a king.

You could save your relationship. If you are single, keep these words in mind—don't let your eccentricities keep you from a relationship if you want one.

- **Flexibility:** Now all you have to do is work on your *flexibility*—and your partner's. And that is no small task, because the bed you want to climb into at night is as personal and enshrouded in mystery as your family on the holidays. (And as full of baggage.) When your partner's needs don't match yours, there's a conflict that has as much to do with avoiding loss as establishing territory. When you or your partner's needs don't match the ideal of "the marriage bed," there's a powerful feeling of loss. Acknowledge it. It's not the end of the world, but denying it may be the end of the relationship. No relationship is perfectly sane or perfectly normal (whatever that is). Accepting the gains is easy. Usually. Once you accept the losses in your bedroom, though, you can begin to have an adult relationship with a loving partner. You can learn to be flexible enough to be that loving partner. And you can relax, knowing your solitude is chosen, not forced on you by your damage.

PRACTICE PAGES

Establishing Safety (Meeting the Gatekeeper)

Some people believe that there are spirit beings in the astral plane that are available to help human beings in a variety of ways. Faith in prayer is one form of this belief, the spirit being in that case being God in particular or saints or angels if your religion incorporates them. If you don't believe in any form of metaphysical reality, this exercise can still benefit you as a construction of the imagination for your own sake (Simpson 1987).

The spirit being you are going to meet is called your Gatekeeper. These entities stand sentry over waking and sleeping, assisting the sleeper's dream journeys. It's up to you to tell your Gatekeeper what kind of protection or assistance you need. You will learn to recognize your personal Gatekeeper by its *energy*. In fact, their names and the way they "look" in your mind's eye, including any assumed gender, may change as you evolve. Spirit energy shapes itself in our own images. You will feel the energy at first by *knowing how your own energy feels,* and feeling the difference between that and your Gatekeeper's nearby. This can be a deepening boundary lesson, helping you to learn the feeling of yourself.

The important thing to remember is that *you* establish a gatekeeper's guidelines; it won't interfere without that conscious agreement from you. The person in the physical body is always the one in charge.

Try this exercise in a quiet but public place, where you can compare the feeling of your gatekeeper's presence with the awareness of other people near you. It will help to record these instructions on tape and play them back in earphones so that you can go forward without having to refer to the book. Once you know how to summon your Gatekeeper and ask for her/his/its assistance, you can better program your sleep and dreaming for the healing and learning—creative problem-solving for example—that comes only from unconscious states

And now, a shamanic visualization to enhance sleep and dreaming. So you'll know how to ask.

1. Sit comfortably in a chair with both feet on the floor. Concentrate on your breath. Let it become slow and steady. Release tension. Get comfortable. Set your intention to meet and greet a spirit

sentry whose job will be to protect the connection between your body/mind and heart/soul.

2. Notice the feeling of your body's energy as you sit quietly in a room. Speak with your *thoughts,* not your voice, so that you become accustomed to the "quiet voice" within. Respectfully ask your beloved Gatekeeper to come near. Continue to breathe deeply.

3. Can you sense a delicate presence? Continue questioning your subtle perceptions while you focus only on your breath, your intention, and the feeling of your body in the room.

4. Ask your Gatekeeper to come close behind you, close enough to feel it/him/her. Continue your meditative focus. Do you "sense" a gender, "see" a body type, "hear" a voice, "feel" a presence? Ask the gatekeeper to help you recognize its presence behind you.

5. When you think you can feel its subtle energy behind you, ask the spirit to noticeably move to your left side. How does it move?

6. Ask it then to move to your right side. Ask the spirit to move away. And then to approach again. Become acquainted with its energy. Learn to feel the difference between its energy near you and your own physical body in the room.

7. You may ask it to do anything to help you know and trust it. Ask for a name, an age, anything it wants to share, its reason for "choosing" you, how to communicate with it, *anything.* Spirit beings are like angels—they want to help. They accept you exactly as you are and want to help you with your soul's goals.

8. Ask it to move in front of you and face you. "Open" your third eye—the intuitive sense in the middle of your forehead that perceives subtle realities. What does your gatekeeper "look" like? Does the form it presents tell you anything about yourself?

9. Tell your Gatekeeper what you need in the way of astral protection in general. For example, you may need emotional boundaries or the right amount of empathy for others' feelings. You can also tell them what you need specifically, regarding dreams, nightmares, night fears, anything. Remember, the spirit will not take any action unless you request it; you are responsible for getting the assistance you need. It will not rescue you, unless you ask for such help. It cannot "read your mind." Speak candidly and listen openly. The safeguards that gatekeepers have to offer can guide you to sleep, help you control, monitor and/or understand your dreams, and introduce you to other spirit helpers, healers, and teachers available to you on the astral plane.

10. Arrange for a shorthand way to summon your helper whenever you want. Such as: *Beloved Spirit, when I close my eyes and call you by name, can you please appear in my mind's eye?* Finally, thank your Gatekeeper by name, remembering always to maintain a feeling of respect between you, and take a moment to gently come out of your meditation. When you are ready, open your eyes.

Using Your Sanctuary

Each night this week, spend some time sitting in your bed before going to sleep, and acquaint yourself with the peaceful place you have created in your bedroom. Breathe.

Write down in a bedside dream journal THREE THINGS you got or learned from your experience of the day—good or bad.

1. _____

2. _____

3. _____

PICK ONE of those that you would like to learn more about. What would you like to know about it? Write that down, too.

After you turn out the light and close your eyes, contact your Gatekeeper. Notice the protective presence your Gatekeeper offers. Ask for the help you need for your sleep time. Ask her/him/it to help you learn about that one thing you chose and wrote about in your journal. Perhaps you'd like a dream with a "teacher," or perhaps a "healer" to help you with the matter. Try to ask for exactly what you need. When you wake, write down your dreams and the kind of sleep you had. How did the help you asked for come to you? Keep practicing and enjoy the permanent, personal retreat that is available to you in your bedroom.

SAFEHOUSE II

Relax. Your house is getting fairly clean. If it's not, you're not working the book. This week, pick one of the rooms we've been through
in the last eight chapters. Explore more deeply the healing potential
there.   Spend some time dreaming, recording your dreams, and
using your dreams to practice taking power over your life. Or . . .
once again, scribble your comments here and unload some of your
anxieties on this and the blank page that follows.

CHAPTER 9

THE PATH OF CONTEMPLATION: LIVING A DAY IN SACRED SPACE

... [T]here are gods of the house, and our daily work is a way of acknowledging these home spirits that are so important in sustaining our lives. To them, a scrub brush is a sacramental object, and when we use this implement with care we are giving something to the soul.

—Thomas Moore, *Care of the Soul**

Putting together a sacred space presents the option of living a sacred life. Not pious, but respectful; not moralistic, but ethical; sacrificing neither wish nor will, but rather experiencing each with reverence. This would suggest a day in which you move through your home as if your life had special meaning. Guess what? It does.

We started this book in the kitchen to establish in your household a pattern of a nurturing and well-nourished life. But we do not usually start a day there. A day begins when you wake up in your own bed, having slept, having dreamt, having fasted for at least—let's hope—eight hours. From this solitary place of sleep, we careen into a day full of other people and activities, which seem to take us away from ourselves. But in actuality, before you return to your sanctuary, you will have expressed yourself differently for each of the different energies of the day. In this chapter you're going to learn to recognize your sacred self even in the midst of those public energies. We'll call them pre-public, peak-public, and post-public times

* The title of this chapter was taken from the same page. Moore attributes the description of housework as "the path of contemplation" to Baltimore astrologer and therapist Jean Lall, who lectures on the subject.

of the day. (Putnam 1983–84). Let's begin at that moment when you realize you're awake.

Take a moment before jumping out of bed. Breathe the spirit of the last lingering bits of sleep and dream "travel" back into your body, tucking your wakening self into your mind as you prepare to face the material world. Put both feet on the floor, "open" the energy centers in your arches, and inhale the power of the planet through them. Stretch your arms and legs and spine, "opening" the chakra on top of your head, and breathe the light from the universe down through it. Let your body awaken to the resources of earth and sky available to all living things.

Next stop, the bathroom, your temple, remember? You do your ablutions here, purifying yourself inside and out. You look at your face in the mirror, setting it right for the day. These are your morning prayers. Take the time to speak your intentions and hopes for this day, honoring your place in the scheme of things.

Now, to the kitchen. You feed yourself and your family with nourishment and the enthusiasm you'll all need to meet the day. Breakfast, juice, coffee, maybe you make lunch for yourself or others. You start the day affirming your confidence that there is plenty in the world to go around, enough for your share to be in reach.

Then it's back to the bathroom and to the bedroom, where you pick up where you left off; finish what you left out. You return to your temple and to your sanctuary to prepare yourself to perform the day's duties with a sacred mind-set. In these places you pull on the costume for the role you play in the world. This uniform presents you masterfully to the rest of the world; it's the "as if" principle at work.

And thus ends the first phase of your sacred day. We'll call it the *pre-public* portion. After this special morning prep time, when your dreams are still on the tip of your mind, if you're like most people, you have to summon the energy to move your day into the public.

You travel, go to work, to school, to the store. You get on the phone with colleagues, clients, or contractors. You interact with ideas, data, materials, or other people. To do this in a sacred way is a twofold task: first, you don't forget who you are inside while engaged in your role as public person; second, you honor the relationship your public role has to your soul's goals. Just as we are not on the planet in physical bodies only to deny them and to withdraw into a spiritual cave, neither do we live in a material world to abstain from pursuing a place in it. Instead, you take your authentic self into that world and proceed *as if* it is sacred.

By lunch, you've merged with your job. Whether you work as a team, in an office, in the field, or alone at home, sometime between noon and three (or the equivalent during any off-hour shift) your work has become your life. You're good at it. You're on the ball. This moment marks the *peak-public* phase of the day.

If you're at home during this phase, you're working in your home office or studio, or pausing from cleaning the house or the laundry to give a thought about what you'll need in the kitchen to prepare tonight's meal. Maybe you're watching *Oprah*, bonding with her soul-seeking audience. Or you could be hosting a working lunch in the dining room. These are the rooms that bring the public home in an authoritative, professional, and formal way.

Then suddenly, it hits you. You're exhausted. That public persona is a lot for anyone to carry. You come home and reconnect with your inner self. Maybe you take a nap, reconvening with your dreams, or eat dinner, rallying yourself with nourishment. You help the kids finish their homework; you water the plants, feed the animals, maybe call a friend on the phone. This daily disconnect from your work life is as important as the earlier connection to it. It signals that you are starting your *post-public* phase of the day. Lots of people call this time "quality time." That means they already see the interactions that happen now as sacred. These are your evening prayers.

Finally you're back in bed, having done your post-public ablutions, turned the lights out, said sweet dreams to your fellow travelers. You write about your day, what you experienced, what you learned, what you need to learn more about. You get ready to connect with your deepest self in sleep. You allow the opportunity to connect with the deepest self of your partner. You sink back into your interior brain where you let the conscious merge with the unconscious. You share the dreamtime with the ones you love. A day lived in sacred space.

That sacred day exists in the perfect world. Yours may not look like that yet, but your house offers many opportunities to approach it. Let's go through it again, more slowly, allowing the various times of the day to draw you to different rooms and to different aspects of yourself, with different potentials for healing your human ailments.

Pre-Public . . . or Before the Day Begins

The Hideout (Closets and Drawers)

You wake up. It's an unstructured day. You're alone. Heaven. You don't have to speak. You think about your dreams. You do your morning routine, shit-shower-shave, tea and crumpets. The important thing is that you suit yourself. You wash. You make your vow: You are going to be clear and wholly true to yourself all day. You go to the closet to choose your clothes for the day. You look in the mirror hanging on the closet door. You look at your clothes. Does being true to yourself and dressing for the public present your first conflict? Hell beckons. If the public wins, down you go: *Who am I?*

Or: It's a regular weekday. Everyone in the family has to get up and be somewhere. Heaven pops like a bubble pricked by the alarm. There is no such thing as *pre*-public. Whoosh. Speaking sucks the memory of any dream adventures right out of your sleepy head. You do your morning routines. Suiting yourself is as foreign a concept as it would be for a member of some pre-agrarian tribe. Your self is tied up with everyone else's. Miraculously, like a creaking machine, everyone gets showered, fed, dressed, and organized. You gulp your coffee with an energy bar. You catch your reflection in the mirror as you brush your teeth. Commitments beckon. Where are you going? Oh, yes, today you're staying home to clean with that book (that's *this* book). You shove everyone out the door. What's this? Silence. You go back to the bedroom; hang the scattered clothes back in the closet. *Who am I?! Now, this is pre-public.*

We're in "the hideout." It speaks to the part of you that is always in the closet—the part you keep private even from your family. But at least *you* should know whom you're hiding in there. Your closets and your drawers are where you can concentrate on the work of being comfortable—or at least familiar—with who you are, *all* the parts of you. It's only you, for crying out loud. Take a quick peek. Look in the mirror on your dresser.

Organize your drawers so they make sense: lingerie, underwear, stockings, socks in the small drawers; separate the shirts and blouses from the trousers and sweaters. If the item is too small, get rid of it—by the time you lose that weight, the styles will be different anyway, and you'll want the new look. On the contrary, if it's too large, you can always belt it. Loose is always in; it's the tight look that comes and goes.

Pick out a favorite item of clothing, one that you feel is "really you." Hang it over the door so you can stand back from it and drink it in. Does it need ironing? Nah. How about mending? If it's a job you can handle, mend it now. If it's not, put it by your house keys and take it to the dry cleaners the *very next time* you go out. Let them mend it. Is it perfect just the way it is? There you are. Sanctuary in the A.M.

The Day Begins

Time to move on. It takes an explosion of energy to go from the private to the public part of the day. It is not a contemplative act. It's extroverted. Most people just close their eyes, hold their breath, and jump—like plunging into a cold pool. Then, they hold their breath for the rest of the day. Travel time revs up that energy for most people. The good thing about long commutes is that they give commuters a chance to remember to breathe.

Even though you are spending this imaginary day at home, to embark on it, you will need a similar expenditure of transitional energy. If you don't have a transit ritual established, use dressing into your work "costume" for that. Work clothes run the gamut from the denim work shirt to the business suit. Put something on to assist you in the ritual of cleaning for sacred space.

The Nerve Center (Home Office/Studio)

More and more people are working at home. And, *working* more at home than ever before. A working home is not so much "where the heart is" as it is where you own the e-mail. Personal computers are becoming almost as ubiquitous as telephones and TVs. By the end of the first decade in the new millennium, they will be standard equipment and everyone will have an office area at home, not just the kitchen drawer of bills next to the phone books, as it was when I grew up. It might be the living room TV, which will drastically change the tone of that room. Better to make a separate office and leave the living room to visiting.

Back then, household management meant planning the daily meals, budgeting the monthly expenses, and, if you were fortunate, putting some savings aside for the future. It was kitchen table stuff—in a sense, digestive. You consumed your income, eliminating it. Today home business is increasingly *neurological.* Messages whiz in and out, creating the need for rapid problem-solving and decisive action; all your life's functions are tied together like a nervous system.

The most popular financial software isn't called "Quicken" for nothing. It's not just fast, the subtext implies, it's revitalizing. And that's not the only word that has changed its meaning through commercial use: "Interactive" used to suggest someone with an outgoing personality, but now it refers to computer software that allows you to communicate with your computer instead of your fellows. How are you keeping up with these changes in the world? Are you resisting them because you fear they will take over your life? How does rebelling against the tide control you? Can you find a balance? Or have you jumped in whole hog? Has it taken over your life? Is your soul becoming digital, or can you still feel yourself winding up and winding down?

Let's face it, very soon, you will be as good as brain-dead without online capability at home—no one will be able to communicate with you, pay you, or process your purchases. Even if you don't invite your colleagues directly into your home office, you will be dealing with them through these cyberspaces. Even if you don't invite Cyberland directly into your head, you will be dealing with it through your colleagues. Where do you stand on the timeline with your work: pre-industrial, industrial, or post-industrial? Hey, are you STRESSED OUT yet?

A friend of mine has an accountant who is a tax lawyer. He keeps a quartz crystal on his desk, next to the computer. It's there to remind him of ancient times when the mathematician was the priest, the sorcerer, and the learned one. Peasants and kings came to these wizards with great questions about how to proceed in their lives and with their business. Whom to marry, when to plant, how to attack, and where to retreat. His crystal reminds him that even today the way people use their money, as shown in their books and receipts, reflects their values, their fears, their strengths and weaknesses, and that they need the care of a priest when faced with the audit of their lives. It must remind him to compose his interactions and financial awareness with the understanding that all interchanges are made of the exchange of energy, because a crystal symbolizes tuning into unseen energies for vision and guidance. (If you can remember the crystal radio set, then you know it's not all woo-woo.) This man's crystal allows him, as a post-industrial professional, to honor a pre-industrial creed.

Whatever creed you bring to your sacred space, it will likely be affected by the environment. Cleaning the office space involves taking care of the lighting, shelves, surfaces, and electronic emissions, each affecting your attitude and maybe your health. If your computer monitor is the regular variety cathode ray terminal (CRT), you are being inundated with emissions. According to Debra Lynn Dadd's *The Nontoxic Home & Office* (1992), we're better off with laptops and flat screens. Their liquid crystal display (LCD) screens emit less radiation than the bigger CRT monitors do, as well as lower levels of positive ion energy, which happens to have a negative effect on the body. She asserts:

High concentrations of positive ions [as found in offices] have been associated with fatigue, metabolic disorders, irritability, headaches, and respiratory problems. In addition, dust, tobacco smoke, and chemical pollutants become positively charged and seek out the nearest grounded or oppositely charged surface, usually the [computer] operator's face. The particles clinging to your face can cause rashes, itchy eyes, and dry skin . . .

—*The Nontoxic Home & Office*, p. 183

Ms. Dadd also suggests you can protect yourself from your PCs electromagnetic fields by getting a grounded screen and, of course, plugging your computer into a properly grounded outlet. I would add, if you use a backup battery device like APCC makes, and a surge protector, you'll protect your data as well. But plants are still the cheapest and prettiest way to counteract unfavorable low-level electromagnetic elements. Emitting desirable levels of *negative* ions through photosynthesis, plants help diminish the static electricity that keeps dust and free-floating anxiety endlessly flying around the room. (Negative ions have a *positive* effect on the body.)

As far as diminishing the unpleasant energies from employers, colleagues, and clients, check your boundaries. The hardest thing to learn is that you can't control others' actions, much less their attitudes; you can only learn to control your response to them. And that's no cheap trick. Choosing to honor the sacred space of work helps when searching for the appropriate response. Delete the junk mail. Forget what you cannot use.

The office at home has particular concerns different from those at work, because it exists in an environment that is probably not equipped like an office building for electrical capacity, lighting, or open space. More than likely, you're working in a nook, not a spacious room, and your papers are in piles everywhere. If your space can't sustain that and still feel sacred to you or your family members, then you need to work on organization and storage. Those issues are the same here as they are in any other room, except here, they rely heavily on file folders. You will also need to invest in a cabinet, or its equivalent, to store them.

I have so many different projects going in my office that the organization is usually three steps behind the creation. I have found, somewhat surprisingly, that such chaos is sacred to my creative being. That presents a problem because my office is also my healing room, which I prefer to be much more orderly, if not spare. The solution would be to have two rooms, but right now, I don't. Therefore, I am challenged to strike a balance that pleases the artist part of me enough to create, while accommodating my obligation to my clients for a clear space in which to make room for their souls' work. This turns out to be not just a storage and organizational problem, but one of discipline as well—namely, keeping current with the paperwork so pile-ups are minimized. I fail frequently, motivating me to work toward a future with those two rooms. We all have these mixed elements that challenge our commitments to family, work, service, and creativity. The discovery of them leads us along the path to "right work." You may find you operate at cross-purposes, as I sometimes do, or you may be one of the fortunate few for whom it all goes smoothly. (But then, you're probably not reading this book.)

As far as cleaning goes, the main problem, here as everywhere, is dust. Papers, books, and static electricity are such friends to dust that it can hardly keep itself away. It used to be that you couldn't vacuum a computer any more than you could a video or cassette tape, because the static erased the data. But that seems to have changed. Perhaps newer computers are more protected from static electricity. At any rate, there are now special hand-sized vacuums for computers, which can be purchased at computer and hardware stores. According to Don Aslett (1993), you can also use the dust attachment on a regular canister model, keeping keyboard and computer dust-free.

The tried and true low-tech method using a cotton swab and a drop of isopropyl (rubbing) alcohol works as well for cleaning keyboards and computer parts as it does for tape heads. I also like the more high-tech style of blasting the dust out with a can of pressurized air (available at most office supply stores). Complete computer cleaning kits with anti-static solution are also available, for those who prefer pre-treated towelettes.

Liquids are the enemy of electronics. Keep it all—coffee, tea, soft drinks, even your expensive imported sparkling mineral water—out of reach of the keyboard. If it gets wet, it's probably dead, so be sparing with your rubbing alcohol and use only a drop, directly applied to the cotton swab, not the instrument. The beauty of alcohol is its rapid evaporation in air, but if you dump it in, it will soak your boards just the same as a glass of water will.

If you do happen to pour fluids into your keyboard, get the corner of a paper towel into the spaces ASAP. Then turn the keyboard over onto more dry towels and used canned air and a hair dryer (not too hot) to blow it dry—and hope the odds are with you. If it's a lost cause, don't worry too much; the average keyboard is not that expensive. But you certainly wouldn't want to have to replace it often.

Of course, prevention is the best bet in this room as in the others. If you vacuum or dust your desk area regularly, you will have less dirt getting into your system. Keep windows closed, especially if dust and pollen are having their way with the outdoors. And suck the cat and dog hair off your office chair and rugs.

As far as the sacred protection of your work, let's start with *rules*. Let your family and anyone else with access to your work space know in very clear terms what they can and can't touch. If children are allowed in the room, give lessons on how to treat the equipment and the information stored on the equipment. A password on your PC locks it from snoops.

In our offices at home, the rule of thumb is basically "Keep Your Mitts Off." I may not be able to keep my office pristine, but somewhere in my mind's eye I have a rough picture of the whereabouts of each piece of paper and paper clip. It could take days to relocate a scrap of vital information if someone even accidentally rearranges this chaos.

To honor the space and the work means having the willingness and ability to be in the space of work wholeheartedly. Even if your "day job" is not your life's work, if it pays your bills, it has value. It takes care of you. To get through a day with a sense of contentment, honor the effort that you give to it right now.

Peak-Public

Sometime between lunch and the afternoon break, you've surrendered to the business of the day and your energy just cooks for productivity. Even your break—if you take one at all—is swamped in the buzz of the outside environment. If you work at night, at home, or spend these working hours alone, you still have this interval of the day. Whether you love your work and "lose" the hours, or hate your job and count them, you can learn to be aware of this shift in your energy. It is when your head is not filled with the issues of your being, but rather with the business of your doing.

The Round Table (Dining Room)

"Let's do lunch." That Hollywood line is not necessarily a brush-off. It's a peak-public reach for connection. It's not so much about eating, though you have to eat. And it's not about being, as a family dinner might be. It's about doing, just as it says. Doing the business of connecting with the public self. In your home, it's the table in your dining room that holds this energy. On this sacred day, you're going to connect that public self to your deepest self, the soul that dines in this sacred space. This business lunch is your big break.

Make the atmosphere congenial, as if you were preparing to dine and to converse—or, if that's too hoity-toity, to eat and to talk—with nothing in the room to distract you from your guest, in this case, you. That means this room works best with plenty of empty space. Set your place across from the Sacred Place Setting you made in the kitchen chapter (chapter 2), the one you've been using to feed your grace. If you haven't done that exercise, put two place settings out. One is for the you that "has it all," the perfect expression of your soul. The other is the place you're going to sit.

Put something lovely on the center of the table. Cut flowers are always nice. Anything that represents your unique aesthetic will work. Serve something simple and tasty; something that looks excellent on a plate and is easy to eat. You wouldn't want to spill spaghetti sauce at your power lunch. Tell yourself how pleased you are that you could come. Receiving this with poise and grace, you may acknowledge that the pleasure is all yours.

The finest dining rooms I have cleaned had in common a large polished table; six chairs; a dark Persian rug (to disguise spills); a buffet, well-stocked with place mats for family and tablecloths for guests, with corresponding, if not identical, cloth napkins; usually a breakfront or china cabinet; simple candlesticks with lovely candles; a striking but not too stimulating piece of art; and a shallow bowl of flowers. And that's it. Spare except for the lively people who filled it with their sterling conversation.

Then again, a lovely expanse of cleared table beckons children, artists, colleagues, and cats, alike, to *utilize* it. So that simple setting is often bestrewn with the business of the day: homework, sewing, blueprints, piles of mail, paw prints. Some of my favorite writers and artists find the dining room table the best place to arrange research, dry canvases, compile a file card index, and storyboard a screenplay. Never mind, this is a working lunch.

What do you talk about at your peak-public lunch with yourself? Your skills, your talents, and the things you've loved doing in your life. Brag. Identify each of your contributions to the world, no matter how small, no matter how long ago or how recent. Notice the new things that have happened since you began this book. Jot them down and pass it across the table like an offer.

And then say something humble. Not a weakness, not a flaw or a failure, but perhaps a tribute to someone who has helped you along the way, or maybe what scares you about the idea of your dreams coming true. What is it that you want to make out of your work life? What do you want to do, to leave behind, that expresses your gift to life, to the world? End your luncheon with sincere thanks for a wonderful meeting. Make a date for a second one. Add new information to your ceremonial plate and cup.

Some days have two peak-public times, separated by a dip in the energy, a mini post-public or a tiny pre-public. For example, when you host or attend a dinner party or other networking function, it's not the same as work, but it's high peak-public. You will have a proper post-public after that.

Until recently, I have mostly had a kitchen table only. Upon it, more often than not, there's been a telephone, a jar of pencils, and various and sundry flyers, announcements, coupons, and lists of things that need to be done, or groceries to be bought. Try as I might to exhort myself or my housemate/s to improve on the upkeep, there is always someone doing more messing than clearing. Peace must prevail in the land—or the meal, to be accurate—so resolve often transmutes to reserve and things are merely shoved aside. Often we remove the meal in its entirety to the living room and eat in front of the tube. So much for the ideal. I tell you this to press the point: The main thing for a peak-public setting is that it is interactive, in a setting that works for the people using it.

A potential snarl is candle wax. Candlelight adds such a wonderfully soft ambience to a dinner, but unless you've thought to get dripless candles, the next day you're scraping the paraffin off the table. You'll think of it next time, won't you? To remove wax from the candlesticks, run them under hot water and the wax will rub off with paper towels as soon as it softens. (Don't let the wax go down the drain.) Then clean or polish the sticks normally.

If wax has dripped onto a tablecloth, pick off the main hunks; what remains you can soak up between several layers of folded newsprint under a hot *iron*. You need enough newsprint to keep the wax from touching the iron, and from soaking through to the ironing board, but not so much that the heat doesn't melt the wax. Press hard and keep blotting both sides with a dry layer. Pay attention to what you're doing or you'll have not only a ruined cloth, but a destroyed iron and ironing surface. Don't iron on the table!

If the wax has hardened directly on the table, chill it with ice and carefully use a *plastic* spatula to scrape up as much of it as you can. Without scratching the finish! Watch out for your fingernails. If you jam a hard piece of wax underneath them, you'll give yourself a torturous wound, triggering a major flashback of some past life bamboo sliver interrogation, if you aren't careful.

TIP: You may be able to disguise a table scratch with the stain of orange pekoe/pekoe black tea. Rub the tea from a boiled teabag into the blemish until the color matches. One of many redemptive qualities of my favorite beverage. Which leads to the sum and substance of making your public meetings divine: high tea. If the company doesn't like it, you don't need them as friends. Well, that's my criteria. What's yours?

Day's End . . . or *Post-Public*

You come home, you eat dinner, and you watch TV. You bring yourself back home in a gradual way. Bathroom, kitchen, living room couch. You visit them all. Most of us wind down well before we hit the sheets, or should anyway. When the day is over but not dead, you ease yourself back to an internal realm. It's often not as private as pre-public, largely because it follows work, rather than sleep. You're not coming out of a dream; you're coming out of a crowd. It consequently offers a different kind of quiet. The noise of the television actually helps many people make the shift. Try some music instead of the TV for a change and see the difference.

Whether you share it or hold it in solitude, it's an honest time. A time to digest the day or the decade. A contemplative time. You will feel its difference from public time because the mask you wear to impress others begins to fall, through sheer exhaustion. You may even notice the exact moment when this shift occurs. For some it's immediately after the door closes on the car parked for the night. For others, not until the kids are in bed. For me, it's when everybody is in bed except me, and my writing day can begin. My favorite time of day.

The Forbidden (Rooms That Aren't Yours)

You go to the kids' rooms to say good night. There's an intimacy being in there that's not just about tucking them into bed. If you're not an imperialist—the lord visiting the serf on their indentured property—then you're an infidel, welcomed in by the grace of love. You may have cleaned this room during the day, put away the toys, picked up the clothes, washed them, put them away. You might have closed the door on the mess. But then, you were an interloper, unsupervised. And part of you knew you were sneaking your moment there. But now, it's in the open, it's all right, it's a moment your child will always remember, hopefully cherish. Check the windows. Say your own prayers, too. Otherwise you don't belong here.

Soon enough, your child needs the same respect for privacy and ownership that you do. Since parenting is an intense tap dance of give and take, bonding and letting go, the most apparent stage for that floorshow is going to be around the child's room. The horror stories I hear from clients about parents who required access to their rooms well into their teens, or who rifled through drawers and possessions in search of infractions, never led to mutually respectful relations in adulthood. If you fear your teenager is taking drugs or collecting weapons, there are ways to find out and confront the situation other than invading their privacy. Educate yourself about the signs of whatever problems your kids face, and then act, armed with information and the strength of your loving character. But I caution against using their rooms as the battlefield between you. I know of no adult who had a parent like that who is okay with it in hindsight. On the contrary, people whose childhood rooms were entered by family members—including parents—only after knocking and receiving permission, have a strong sense of their own boundaries as well as other people's. My general opinion is when they're big enough to open and close their own doors, the kids are old enough to take care of their own rooms, too. To their taste, I might add. If you don't like the way it looks, close their door.

Then there's your spouse's office or your housemate's den. Maybe they've gone into it to wind down alone. The important thing to remember is, *this room is not yours.* That means you don't have to live in it, and you are only a guest with regard to it. Now, what conflicts do these factors present? For housemates there should be none, unless they are attracting vermin and pestilence with their filth. Then you've got a problem. But since the Health Department is on your side, you've got leverage where it counts. Why should it be any different when the rooms of partners are concerned? If there is conflict here, it should be obvious that the real deal is the dynamic in the relationship between you. Here again, look to the precious gift in the phrase "a room of one's own."

Your partner is an adult. If you are lucky enough in your family to have rooms of your own, let that adult be responsible for their own room. The room is sacred to this person you love. If your family agreement is that you are the one to clean it, you must negotiate how that's going to happen. Try forging a contract for the conditions under which you (or they) will keep it. Once it's been done, it's your job to leave it alone. It's their room. Here is a place to bargain your cleanliness values for the house as a whole. If socks and clothes and clutter have carte blanche in one room, better to keep them off the bathroom, living room, and bedroom floors. Everyone needs to have this kind of sacred space. In lieu of a whole room of one's own, perhaps you can negotiate a corner of one's own, for the same purposes. And leave it alone in a sacred way. Can you let it be their business?

The Courtyard (Decks, Stoops, Patios, and Porches)

For some, a perfect evening is spent watching the sunset. The moonrise. You have a smoke out on the porch. You sit with the dog. Hanging out on the patio was my image of California when I moved here fifteen years ago from the Northeast. But no one has time for it. I have since learned as well that single family home dwellers are not supposed to sit on front porches anymore. Apparently, they are only for show. If you want to be outside, the Welcome Wagon seems to say, get in the back. Too bad. I like the front. I like to wave hello to the folks walking their dogs, having their jog, and the like. This post-public time is fast deteriorating into post-community. And that is *not* a good thing.

I say, defy it. Say good night to the day on the porches of North America and re-enliven the neighborhood. This is how neighbors become friends, friends become extended family, and family members become close companions. Sitting in the gloaming. Dancing in the courtyard. Lounging on the deck. Singing on the stoop. Talking deep into the night on a screened-in porch. This is precious time. As sacred to the feeling of community as bedtime is to your feeling of sanctuary.

If you don't know what I'm talking about, you are suffering from what Studs Terkel calls "our national Alzheimer's disease" (1996). You have no memory of the way previous generations lived, when folks weren't scared of everything from drive-by shootings to unstructured time. They used to hang out alone or with friends and family, and just *be* inside that time. It wasn't so much about making plans as about telling stories, or *lies* as they used to call them.

Some people still do this sort of thing, kicking back with lemonade, a beer, or a hot cup of coffee, dancing with grandparents, nieces, and nephews. But more and more they are considered loafers and losers. Whether they are or not has nothing to do with the upkeep of this space. When you use it, you are more likely to keep it clear of cobwebs. The same is true about close friends, family, and even the workings of your own inner mind.

Sweep! The floors of a courtyard, deck, or porch are usually built of cement, brick, stone, or unfinished wood. A stiff broom is the best bet for their rugged and crumbling natures. If yours is outside, and you live where water is plentiful, hose it down; if you live in a drought area, sweeping is plenty. Inside, a wet mop does it justice. Basically it's the same deal as the basement in terms of cleaning, right down to weeding the cracks (although maybe that was just our basement). Do you tend to take this area for granted? Do you spend time with yourself or someone else, letting the day come down? Finding the sense of the years? Whether you have only a fire escape landing or a big old wrap-around porch, this part of your home is an extension of your relaxed soul. It's not about attainment; it's about enjoying the continuity of your life. It's the garden counterpart to the living room, built with the materials of the basement. You do the analysis.

In Holland—the stereotype is true—front steps get scrubbed. For comfortable street-watching from the stoop, and a clean rear end when you're done, it's a great custom. This isn't a public corner or someone else's responsibility. This outside living room needs your proprietorship to remain unspoiled. Scrape off the gum, collect the cigarette butts—whether or not you tossed them there—and discard them. Don't let people use your threshold as a trash bin. Prune what you don't want growing there and set down the roots of what you do want.

Outside porch furniture gets gritty and sticky from the elements as well and takes some straightforward attention. You want things you can brush off well with a dry sponge or wash with soap and water. Similarly, an old friend who can't be hosed down now and then when they get funky will not go the distance. On the other hand, neglect and misuse will rot in like manner furniture, friendship, and faculties to the core.

Now, Go to Bed

Finally, it's over. One day lived in the consciousness that there's more to being than reason implies, than rationality counts. Put away the remote, fold the sofa blanket. Fluff the cushions on the couch. Check for change that's dropped out of pockets. If you find any, take it as a good omen: Change *is* as good as a rest. Now off to your sanctuary. Hold your own soul and your significant other close. Give thanks for the light and the dark in this day. Rest. Sleep and dream of magical meanings. When morning comes, the darkness will be light.

PRACTICE PAGE

When you started the process in this book, you had the opportunity to rate the state of clean and sacred in your space. Now that you've thought so much more about how you relate to your rooms and what the state of clean means, here is the chance to chart your changes regarding them. You'll find a couple new ideas thrown in for good measure.

Charting the Clean-up *Revisited*

1. As in chapter 1, let's look at the whole, and see how it charts now. Again, we're going to arbitrarily use the number 5 for the proverbial five minutes it will take to do each task listed below for six rooms, except where another amount of time is indicated in parentheses like so: (10), (15), or (20), meaning minutes. To remind you, if you need to do *each task* indicated to clean, for example your bedroom, listed below as (a), your personal time (pt) for that room will equal the full Total Time of 60 minutes (pt=TT=60), which is about the longest a bedroom should take to clean. If, on the other hand, you only need to make the bed, your personal time will be five minutes. (pt=5)

    A. **Bedroom:** Shoes, hangers, hanging clothes, folding clothes, drawer organization (10), floor (15), bed, overall room aesthetics (10); TOTAL TIME (TT)= 60 minutes (will rate a 10 on the chart);

    B. **Home Office:** Papers, filing (10), equipment and cords, bills (10), room efficiency, TT=35;

    C. **Living Room/Den:** Dust, dirty dishes and other clutter (10), floors and rugs (15), decor, furniture (under the cushions too), cozy/comfy quotient, TT=45;

    D. **Dining Room:** Table, empty space, cooking/serving accessories, room clear of extras, crumbs and sticky dregs, beauty and tranquility, TT=30;

    E. **Porch:** Dirt, weeds, bugs, greenery, furniture, delightfulness, TT=30;

    F. **Kitchen:** Dishes (10), counters, cabinets, stovetop, oven (20), refrigerator (15), sink, floor (15), TT=90;

    G. **Bathroom:** Bathtub/shower (10), basin and accessories (10), toilet, mirrors/chrome, towels, clutter, floor/walls (10), TT=50.

2. Now, the chart. Once again, you'll rate whether each room will take a short amount of time to clean (1) or a long time (10). If your personal time equals the total time (pt=TT) then the room rates a maximum 10 on your chart. The rate for needing to do only one task is 1. Draw a vertical bar on the graph below to show how you rate your rooms on that scale.

3. Remember that each room has a corresponding sacred relationship to a particular area of your life. In a nutshell, they could be seen as: **(a)** self and partner, **(b)** role in the world, **(c)** being and visiting, **(d)** meeting and greeting, **(e)** kicking back with refreshing beverages, **(f)** nurturance, and **(g)** ablutions. How does the correlation look at this point now that you've nearly finished the exploration of your home in this way? Rate yourself as you see fit and chart a line in a different color alongside the corresponding bar to show the comparison. You may be surprised by what you see. This graph will show your progress and give you an idea of what areas you still need to concentrate on in your house, and those areas of your life that still need healing.

Healing House Bar Graph

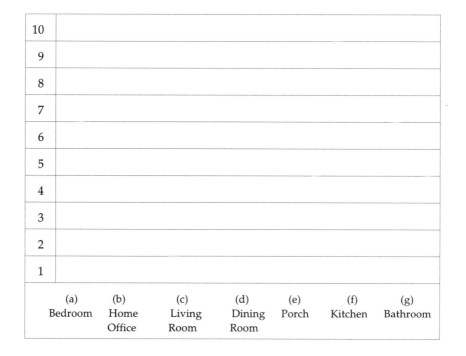

Freewriting: Charting your Day by Haiku

This exercise asks you to try your hand at writing haiku. This Japanese poem form is a wonderful tool to help you get in touch with your own internal rhythms and shifting perspectives that cycle in a day as your environment affects you (Putnam 1983–84). A haiku poem has no more than seventeen syllables in a total of three lines. It strives to tell a story by describing a single image. The first line has five syllables, the second has seven, and the third has five again. Modern, "lowbrow" haiku poems written about everyday issues are called *senryu.* Here is an example:

> The red wagon's wheel,
> shiny, bent, and over there—
> a thumb in the mouth.

For at least one week, sit down and free-write a haiku at each of the three times of the day discussed in this chapter. Don't spend a lot of time, don't think a lot, don't limit yourself, don't count the syllables until after you have written it. As your experience grows, you will get closer to the seventeen. Just write in three short lines the feeling of the moment. The way it looks. Or the way it sounds or smells or feels. You are using this exercise to learn something new about your own sacred rhythms that rock and roll your day.

- **Pre-Public:** While you are still in your private head space; before you have entered the world of others. If you have a hectic household, then the best time to free-write this initial haiku would be before you leave your bed or while in the bathroom first thing in the morning.

- **Peak-Public:** When you take your midday break at the "high noon" of your day, or just a tad later, whenever you feel that happening. Take a minute and free-write a senryu that describes the feeling or point of view of this time.

- **Post-Public:** After the day is done; it may be after work, or not until you curl up with a book before bed. You will start to notice *the very moment* you shift into the second private time of the day, after you've been "in the world."

You may find some days have two complete cycles, or a doubling up of one of the time periods. If you work two jobs for example, or if you go out for the evening. Write your haiku for the "second day," too. If you have a lot of these, maybe now you understand why you feel like you're living a double life ... and why you are so tired!

CHAPTER 10

DOING NOTHING: NOT CLEANING

. . . dare to be idle . . .

—Brenda Ueland, *If You Want to Write*

Sometimes you have to take a break from working on your life. And your house. Sometimes the most important thing you can do for your overall health is *nothing*. After all, you can't just keep making sacred things and doing sacred chores. You have to remember to make *space* before you fill it with anything. The way you make space is by *not* doing. With mindfulness. A musical score shows the symbol for "rest" when the composer wants the time to be held with *no* music played. Graphic designers block out areas for "white space" to surround, and thereby emphasize, the printed areas. This chapter's reason for being is the same. To organize a time for nothing.

Brenda Ueland, an early-twentieth-century journalist, well-known for her 1936 book on writing (still in print, by the way), had a word for this kind of not doing: *moodling*. Unlike its twin, "footling," which is a real word meaning "idle foolishness," moodling had a method to its madness. Doing nothing gets your mind to let its hair down and find its way to something from the Infinite. Permission granted to moodle.

This doing nothing is not the doing nothing of being unable to move from exhaustion, illness, or alienation from your life. Not that. Not the nothing of depression or chronic fatigue immune deficiency syndrome where even nothing feels like too much to do. Not a low-down, can't get out of bed, the self-esteem so low, the floor looks up, kind of nothing. This doing nothing is a glorious acceptance of the chaos that life needs before it can organize itself into *something*. A break in the journey. Playing hooky. Vegging out. Calling in well. Taking a mental health day. Or week. Or year.

The growing field of child counseling is learning about the benefits of unstructured play in the healing process. Anybody who works with kids knows you can hardly communicate with one if you don't know how to play, making it the better part of teaching, learning, finding out, explaining. Granted, play is not exactly doing nothing, but for most of us, it feels like it. That's because both play and nothing are things adults in Western society are not supposed to do. This is not sports, which can be just another way to strive, a competitive acrostic for work, war, and winning. We're talking about purposeless playfulness. Permission hereby granted to play in your time off.

Maybe you'd rather call it "puttering." Studies are showing that unstructured (in)activity can create an open space in your thinking that jumps you past mental ruts, allowing new ideas to pop into awareness from nowhere. Meditators strive for "empty mind," getting the mind to *think* nothing. Only then, is it quiet enough to hear the Universe being. What's great about *playing*—which doing nothing at all lacks—is the endorphin boost it lends to your mood.

So, let it all go. Your worries, your clutter, your commitments. For now, just forget about them. Perhaps an important aspect of your life or your home will be revealed when you have the distance and the downtime to see it again fresh. I understand this may not be easy. A break can be fraught with anxiety and worry. Puttering can get your mind off those. You can also read a book, catch up on the Sunday paper, play Scrabble with your best pal, or pet your cat. Julia Cameron in *The Artist's Way* goes one step further. She suggests a week of no reading at all. It's a whole week dedicated to finding out what you feel and think, without the crutch of "expert opinion" or the pressure of other people's viewpoints, or even the distraction of external crises, dramas, and stories. You don't have to go that far; this is supposed to be fun. Let this week of not cleaning offer you the freedom to find something out about yourself that feels good. Can you stand that?

My original intention was to quote studies on the benefits of play, puttering, and inactivity. To quote Zen. To defend the proposition by offering such evidence that explains why free time is a good thing. But asking you to read all that is just way too much work, to justify doing nothing. So I offer you this:

Banausic: *adj.: relating to or concerned with earning a living*—used pejoratively.

—Merriam Webster's 365 New Words
Calendar (June 16, 1999)

Apparently the ancient Greeks did not value work as much as we do today; they believed it prevented important things like thought and conversation. Henry David Thoreau felt the same way. Because of that he was able to create one of the classics of American literature, *On Walden Pond*. As did the twentieth century's bohemians, who spawned more great writing, popularized great jazz, and brought black berets to the masses. But the economic politics of the last twenty years have looted free time and put everyone to work. Well, the economy's good again and I propose we rekindle such moodling spirit! It may empty the pockets, but it fills the heart, the soul, and the mind.

Therefore, what follows are some *Un*-Practices, some *anti-banausic* exercises in case doing nothing is beyond your imagination. But I welcome you to ignore them. Relax. Let life finds its way in the chaos that it loves.

PRACTICE PAGE

Un-Exercises for the Anti-Banausic

Listening, Hanging Out, Going Fallow, and Stopping Dead in Your Tracks

These *non-activities* are merely guidelines permitting you to waste time with conviction. Feel free to ignore them and do nothing on your own terms.

1. Sit on your front stoop for an hour or so and say hello to everyone who happens by. Add the enjoyment of a favorite beverage if you like.

2. With a pen and pad of paper beside you, sit for twenty minutes somewhere that is safe enough to do so *with your eyes closed* (no muggers, no mountain lions, no foul balls). Jot down as many different sounds as you can identify. Don't worry about neatness.

3. Drawing one continuous line, connect the first letters of every word that describes a *sound*, written on the pad from the previous exercise. Drawing a second line, connect the last letters of each sound word. Color in the loops that are formed by the connected sound nouns. Why? No reason. Just make a picture without merit. This used to be called FUN.

4. Go to an art museum. While there, enter the bathroom and rate it on a scale of 1–10 for comfort, cleanliness, and aesthetics. How does it compare to yours? How would your favorite artist represented in these halls re-do it if he/she could? Leave a note.

5. Invite a friend (or three) on a play-date that has absolutely no redeeming social value. Something like miniature golf, boogie boarding, or a virtual reality amusement park. If there's something silly you've always wanted to do, do it now.

CHAPTER 11

POLISHING THE FINISH

What we call style is an expression of our inner being.

—Eugenio Zanetti, 1999

If you have followed the prescriptions in this book, both your house and your life have become more sacred to you, not to mention clean. Of course, since you took the last week off, it might need some attention. So, here we go again. The Sacred is a constant taskmaster. Like the proverbial *women's work*, it's never done.

But maybe you've only read the book and not cleaned your home, room by sacred room; and neither have you done any of the other exercises. Worse yet, you may have just skimmed. I hope you don't think you know from a quick read what it feels like to heal your soul or clean your house, recreating them in sacred space. To really know, you have to do the deeds.

Creating sacred space in which to live a healing life is, in fact, a lifelong process. The question for any of us becomes: How can I make it pleasurable? How can I make it meaningful? How can I make it real? For me, it's about finding the magic and the mystery of life on a regular basis. Finding the sacred in everyday life. And making it a part of my house.

How You Know You're Done

How do you know when your house is a genuine Sacred Space? You certainly don't want to be living in a church. It has to be a lot more comfortable and a lot less righteous. You might also ask: How do you know when you're healed? You don't want to be waiting for a total absence of aches, pains, or problems. You can't cure life. How do you know when you're done? In a word, when you feel at home in your house, in your body, in your life. When you are expressing your inner being somewhere in a style that brings you satisfaction.

Your house is becoming sacred space if you are more comfortable in your own skin there. If you don't have to leave it to find your heart, your own mind, your conscience. If being in it is helping you learn to manage your fear, listen to your anger, comfort your sadness, and wait out your faithlessness. If it gives you back the courage to take your whole (or partial) self out to meet the world. You are healing in sacred space if you are broadening your options, extending your *range of emotion*.

It's easy to tell when your house is clean. It has energy. Light seems to float in the air, lifting the whole room like a buoy. The furniture seems to tell you where it belongs. Walls keep your confidences. Floors support their weighty subjects, rather than pulling you to your knees with a scrub brush. Appliances sparkle and electronics twinkle, blinking the praises of modern technology. Outsiders become welcome. At last there is room for them. Whether or not life is perfect, your house is showing you what wellness looks like. Today you can recognize it.

My college friends and I used to "call it done" when the woefully deficient dormitory dryers had dried our clothes dry *enough*. I first heard the wisecrack, "Good enough for government work," from stagehands building flimsy theatrical sets that looked completely real. I still find these low-standard quips user-friendly. I call my house clean when I can see the surfaces again and still know where my stuff is. Good enough is an important phrase to know for both cleaning and healing. Because here is the real truth: You're never done once and for all. That old axiom about women's work may be sexist and maddening, but it has wisdom in it and might explain why older women live longer and healthier lives than older men. Cleaning, cooking, and creating the good life never reaches retirement. Perfection is not attainable. Progress is made in constant tiny steps. You may as well make them a spiritual practice, and seek your wisdom in the thankful ordinary. Whistle while you work. . . .

No matter how well you've cleaned, much of it will need to be redone in a week or so, dishes daily or more often, the bigger jobs less often, but even so. It ceases to be so depressing when you come to terms with the idea that you choose your own standard, your own aesthetic, and you maintain it at whatever level you have the energy for, when you have the energy for it, or the money for it, if you can afford help. The same is true of healing, and of your relationship with your sacred spirit.

Polishing Up—One Last Look

When you've finished cleaning your house, sweep through one last time with all your antennae up, looking for what's been left out. Give the mirrors and chrome a once-over, rubbing away any missed or forgotten streaks. Do the same with the electronics and the windows. Rub your last clean cloth over the fine wood furniture; pick up any lint, strings, or pieces of sponge that have been left behind; smooth out your footprints on the carpet. If there are big jobs you didn't have time for, make a note to schedule time before the next big holiday.

When you've finished cleaning your house, take care that you are leaving your equipment clean and in its assigned place. This is important because concentrated grime corrodes whatever it's attached to. Any and all remains of hair, dust, and debris must be cleared from the sink and drains, pulled off the vacuum attachments. Make sure you have rinsed and squeezed the sponges and mops, and tossed the rags into the laundry basket. Cleaning products should be collected and put away without drips or clogs, their lids closed up tight. See that nothing remains unfinished unless you have chosen to leave it that way. Take a good long look—when your house is clean, it *looks* clean—and breathe in the air you have made fresh.

But How Do I Know if *I'm* DONE?!

Make the comparison. When the house is done, it will look better. So will you feel better when you are done. When you are in better shape, you're also going to feel better about your life. It's just like healing from any wound, really. Becker and Selden explain in *The Body Electric* (1985) how an injury heals. For a while after the first sharp pain, the nerves feel numb, a result of a rush of neurotransmitters with a positive charge. (Interestingly enough, positive impulses *numb*.) This helps the body regroup so you can make important decisions and prepare to heal. Once the healing begins, the nerves stream a negatively charged "current of injury" that stimulates the growth of new tissue. The blood sends white blood cells to protect these new cells from infection.

This negatively direct current of neurotransmitters, along with the fighting blood cells, causes those aches, pains, and itching of healing wounds. The worse the injury, they say, the more negative energy goes to heal it. So you see, not all negative energy is bad. Sometimes it's growing a new you. That explains a little bit about the pain and the anguish that often goes with healing your life, too. It bears repeating, *you have to feel it to heal it.*

But when the injury is well, according to *The Body Electric*, it settles into a neutral zone, showing equal parts positive and negative ions. That explains why wellness does not feel all blissful and you high as a kite. Think about the last time you had a headache. You were very aware of your head when it hurt, but when it was healed, you didn't even notice your head anymore, did you? Healthy feels *regular*. You are no longer thinking about healing. This keys you in to the end of the process.

If you are getting bored with your healing work, take an inventory. Be excruciatingly honest and check your current or overall state against the conditions listed below. These are the conditions that should exist if you've been taking your life and your healing seriously enough to change what you could, and lightly enough to let go of what you couldn't.

Healing Checklist

☐ Support is available to you; phone numbers are current, important relationships are in order.

☐ Your Personal Emergency Alternative Resources List (PEARL) is up-to-date for who you are today. You know how to help yourself in an emergency.

☐ Your relationship to food, medicines, and other self-care substances is manageable; you have what you need on hand.

☐ You have had ample practice dealing with your major emotional issues, phobias, fears, and injuries. You may not have achieved mastery over your life, but you are aware of what you are working on, and you are functioning satisfactorily on a day-to-day level.

☐ You are in touch with your addictions and in recovery for those that have made your life unmanageable; that is, you are clean, sober, and taking it easy, one day at a time.

☐ You are in daily dialogue with Spirit (whether you consider that God or your own Creativity is your business), knowing that going there for guidance regarding your enlightened self-interest is preferable to reacting out of some ideological obedience.

☐ You have some methods at your disposal to help you let go of things you can't control and feeling/thought patterns that eat away at your insides.

☐ You are aware of how long you can stay in limbo about an issue without going insane. You have gained comfort with delayed gratification, increased endurance in waiting for a conclusion, and can sit still, patient with unknown quantities, but you are not paralyzed to indecision or inaction.

☐ You at least know what a good boundary is, even if you are not always adept at holding yours or seeing others'. But you're getting there.

☐ While working to increase your strengths and decrease your limitations, you are aware of your limits and can respect them. You also accept that other people have limitations.

☐ You accept yourself as a sexual being and do not need to associate sexuality with shame or with power. Your exploration of all three of these qualities—often linked—is ongoing.

☐ You allow yourself to dream—both in terms of hopes for your desired future as well as in your sleeping life—with honesty, openness, and willingness. That which is difficult for you in this area, whether it is sleeping, imagining, or intimacy, you can acknowledge to yourself and to at least one other, and you are willing to delve into your own psyche to develop more ease there.

☐ You are not merely a product of your parents' effect on you. You have moved beyond them, accepting that they have their own path to follow and you have yours. When painful things arise in you regarding the messages that were implanted in your brain during your childhood, you have tools to help you dig them up, compost them, transplant them, or graft them to something more useful. You are practiced at taking the time to do this work, and not letting it overpower your life.

☐ You don't spend much time doing things you'd rather not do with people you'd rather not do it with. This is not to say that you are unwilling to undertake unpleasant tasks that are necessary to maintain your home, family, community relationships, profession, and the job at hand. You are willing and able to do whatever is necessary to keep these things in good order. But your interest in them incorporates your interest in you.

☐ You have grown in emotional "intelligence." You are more armed than before with the tools, techniques, methods, and instruments of change. Your bookshelves and your address book are full of people, places, and ideas that can assist you in getting your changing needs met. When you don't have what you need, you can find out how to get it. You have a variety of avenues to try when one doesn't pay off immediately and you have the stamina to keep trying "when at first you don't succeed."

☐ You don't depend on one person to meet all your needs. You allow your significant other, best friend, or therapist to have their own needs, and to be imperfect in handling yours. You have different people to call on for different aspects of your personality and interests—interactions with colleagues, recreational companions, and other familiars offer you at least some degree of satisfaction. Conflicts here don't kill you, nor do you seek them.

☐ You are able to meet your basic needs. To paraphrase the song, *Your life is / more than your work is: / your work is / more than your job. . .* (King 1977). You are learning about balance.

☐ You pursue inspiration; you don't wait around for it to drop in.

☐ The main thing is this: When you notice you are feeling, thinking, and being negative, you recognize that something's up for you and you spend the energy to use it for healing, destroying only that which needs destroying and constructing only that which wants constructing. You allow the healing to happen, the new limb, as it were, to grow. Then you let in positive energy to arbitrate, smooth things out, and plant the seeds for a positive future.

If you can check off most of these conditions, you should be thrilled. Congratulate yourself. Take a vacation. You are healing in sacred space.

If this list helped you see which wounds are still smarting, that's good, too. A commitment to lifelong learning about your humanity doesn't ask you to be done healing in six weeks or even six years. It does ask you to keep working on the sacred in your space.

So, whether you're done or not, you should cherish yourself with pride. You trudged, slipped, or fell to the basement and climbed back up, finding your soul expressed in everything you do, more powerful, more yourself than before, and with all the promise that a cherished soul is entitled to. Your life belongs to you. It's a house you've paid off. I am honored to have walked this way with you and to have shone a light, however dimly. The wounded ones seeking meaning, the ones who get up and lick those wounds into new flesh and bone, into strong hearts and open minds, you are the ones who, saving yourselves, save the world, making it a sacred space for all of us. Welcome to that citizenry. We have been waiting for you.

PRACTICE PAGE

Moving On

Imagine that you are standing at the door of a mountain cabin. You are facing *out* into the morning light. It is the first warm day of the season. The air sparkles like dew on the fresh green. You reach into your pocket for your sunglasses and pull out a map you didn't even know was there. It's a map of the road to your *IDEAL LIFE*. All you have to do now is follow it.

1. Make a picture of that map. Draw it like it's a treasure map, only the treasure is more than riches; it's everything your soul wants, your own Personal Paradise. Use colors, collage, whatever fulfills your ideal. Be greedy. Be bold. Savor the time you spend drawing this map to your ideal life. These are your hopes and wishes. Put it away for twenty-four hours. Then come back and do the next step.

2. Twenty-four hours later, take a look at the map to your dream life. You don't believe in it, do you? Okay, add onto it all the obstacles, pitfalls, and ambushes that you have encountered before or expect to encounter, blocking your way, impeding your progress (walls, traps, bad weather, accidents, you name it). Glue things on if you want. Be sad, be angry, be resentful. Put everything on it that you think could or will block the way to your Ideal Life. (If you want your original map to be unsullied, copy it *in color* and use the duplicate for this exercise.) These are your doubts and fears. Again put it away for twenty-four hours.

3. On the third day, it's time for some magic. There are no obstacles that can't be overcome *if* you have the proper tool for the proper job. What tools or equipment would help you get over, under, around, or through the obstacles, pitfalls, and ambushes blocking you to your rich life? Put them on the map. Draw, cut, paste, fantasize, fabricate—whatever you need to provide a way beyond the blockades in your path as you've drawn it. Bridges, tunnels, helicopters, power tools, genies, invisible doors, miracles, nothing is too fantastic or unrealistic for this exercise. This is how reality is created. Call upon the image; let substance find the way. And the walls came a-tumbling down. . . .

4. Now for the mystery. Turn your map over to its blank back. Using a pair of scissors, without drawing an outline, without even looking, snip yourself out of the map like a paperdoll cut-out. Draw

your face and color yourself in on that blank side. Now, turn it back over to the other side. That side's your colorful soul, the part created in sacred space. Put the freed spirit on your altar. It will lead you down the road of your dreams. Where you are the sacred star.

REFERENCES

Aslett, Don. 1993. *The Cleaning Encyclopedia*. New York: Dell Trade Paperback (Bantam Doubleday Dell).

———. 1984. *Clutter's Last Stand*. Cincinnati, Ohio: Writer's Digest Books.

Aslett, Don, and Laura Aslett. 1986. *Make Your House Do the Housework*. Cincinnati, Ohio: Writer's Digest Books.

Bartlett, John. 1992. *Bartlett's Familiar Quotations*, sixteenth edition. Edited by Justin Kaplan. Boston: Little, Brown and Company.

Bass, Ellen, and Laura Davis. 1993. *Beginning to Heal: A First Book for Survivors of Child Sexual Abuse*. New York: HarperPerennial.

———. 1988. *The Courage to Heal: A Guide for Women Survivors of Child Sexual Abuse*. San Francisco: Harper & Row.

Becker, Gavin de. 1997. *The Gift of Fear*. New York: Little, Brown & Co.

Becker, Robert, and Gary Selden. 1985. *The Body Electric: Electromagnetism and the Foundation of Life*. New York: Quill/William Morrow.

Bradshaw, John. 1990. *Homecoming: Reclaiming and Championing your Inner Child*. New York: Bantam.

———. 1988. *Healing the Shame That Binds You*. Deerfield Beach, Fla.: Health Communications, Inc.

Bronte, Charlotte. 1966. *Jane Eyre*. Harmondsworth, Middlesex, England: Penguin Books. First published 1847.

Brown, Denslow. 2000. "The Organizer Coach." Professional Web site at www.organizercoach.com.

Bruch, Hilde. 1978. *Golden Cage: The Enigma of Anorexia Nervosa*. New York: Vintage Books.

Bruyere, Rosalyn. 1989. *Wheels of Light: A Study of the Chakras*, Vol. 1. Sierra Madre, Calif.: Bon Productions.

Bruyere, Rosalyn. 1986–1990. Founder and Director of the Healing Light Center Church (and mystery school), Sierra Madre, California. Workshops, lectures, and personal communications.

Campbell, Joseph, with Bill Moyers. 1988. *The Power of Myth*. New York: Doubleday.

Campbell, Joseph. 1973. *The Hero with a Thousand Faces*; third paperback printing. Princeton, N.J.: Princeton/Bollingen. Ananda K. Coomaraswamy quote is from *Hinduism and Buddhism*, (New York: The Philosophical Library, no date), 6–7.

Cameron, Julia. 1992. *The Artist's Way*. Los Angeles: Jeremy P. Tarcher.

Chapman, Eugenia, and Jill C. Major. 1991. *Clean Your House and Everything in It*. New York: Perigee.

Chrisman, Miriam. 1980–84. Personal conversations. Northampton, Mass.

Cobb, Linda. 1998. *Talking Dirty with the Queen of Clean*. New York: Pocket Books.

Compton's Interactive Encyclopedia. 1994, 1995. Compton's NewMedia, Inc. Cambridge, Mass: Softkey International, Inc.

Dadd, Debra Lynn. 1992. *The Nontoxic Home & Office*. Los Angeles: J. P. Tarcher.

The Dalai Lama (His Holiness, Tenzin Gyatso, the fourteenth Dalai Lama). 1991. *Path to Bliss: A Practical Guide to Stages of Meditation*. Edited by Christine Cox and Thubten Jinpa. Ithaca, N.Y.: Snow Lion Publications, 34.

Dreamscape. 1984. Directed by Joseph Ruben. Starring Dennis Quaid, Kate Capshaw, et al. Los Angeles: Image Entertainment.

Elizabeth I. From David Hume's 1759 *History of England Under the House of Tudor*, vol. II, ch. 7. In *Bartlett's Familiar Quotations*, sixteenth edition; Justin Kaplan, gen. ed. (Boston: Little, Brown and Co. 1992), 145:3.

Estes, Clarissa Pinkola. 1992. *Women Who Run with the Wolves*. New York: Ballantine.

Ferguson, Marilyn. 1997. *Brain/Mind: A Bulletin of Breakthroughs*. Los Angeles: Interface Press.

Fiffer, Sharon Sloan, and Steve Fiffer, eds. 1995. *Home: American Writers Remember Rooms of Their Own*. New York: Vintage Books (Random House).

Finster, Elaine Jay. 1991. *Health, Wealth, & Balance Through Feng Shui.* Bailey, Colo.: New Age Concepts.

Gilman, Charlotte Perkins. 1973. *The Yellow Wallpaper.* New York: The Feminist Press at the City University of New York. First published 1892.

Goldberg, Natalie. 1994. *Long Quiet Highway.* New York: Bantam.

———. 1990. *Wild Mind.* New York: Bantam.

———. 1986. *Writing Down the Bones.* Boston: Shambhala Publications.

Good Vibrations and the Sexuality Library Catalogue. No date. San Francisco: Open Enterprises. 1 (415) 974-8980.

Graham, Barbara. 1994. *Women Who Run with the Poodles.* New York: Avon.

Gramling, Elizabeth. 1989–1995. Personal conversations. Pasadena, Calif.

Heloise. 1992. *Heloise from A-Z.* New York: Perigee.

———. 1989. *All-New Hints from Heloise.* New York: Perigee.

Henley, William Ernest (1849-1903). Invictus. In *Bartlett's Dictionary of Quotations*, sixteenth edition, Justin Kaplan, gen. ed. (Boston: Little, Brown and Co. 1992), 557:10.

Highwater, Jamake. 1981. *The Primal Mind: Vision and Reality in Indian America.* New York: Harper & Row.

Hillman, James. 1983. *Inter Views: Conversations with Laura Pozzo on Psychotherapy: biography, love, soul, the gods, animals, dreams, imagination, work, cities, and the state of the culture.* Woodstock, Conn.: Spring Publications, Inc.

Impact Personal Safety/Prepare, Inc., self-defense training system. 1-800-245-KICK.

Ingerman, Sandra. 1991. *Soul Retrieval: Mending the Fragmented Self.* San Francisco: HarperSanFrancisco.

Kent, Cassandra. 1997. *Organizing Hints and Tips.* New York: DK Publishing, Inc.

King, Charlie. 1977. "Our Life Is More Than Our Work." Pied Asp Music (BMI).

Kolodny, Nancy. 1987. *When Food's a Foe.* Boston: Little, Brown and Co.

Lam Kam Chuen. 1996. *Feng Shui Handbook: How to Create a Healthier Living and Working Environment.* New York: Henry Holt and Co.

Lane, Phil. 1988. Transformational Ceremony Workshop. Los Angeles: Healing Light Center Church.

Leonard, Linda Schierse. 1990. *Witness to the Fire: Creativity and the Veil of Addiction*. Boston: Shambhala.

Mann, Nicholas R. 1996. *The Dark God: A Personal Journey through the Underworld*. St. Paul, Minn.: Llewellyn Publications.

Meyer, Richard E. 1995. Julia understands everything. *Los Angeles Times Magazine*. December 17, 20.

Moore, Thomas. 1992. *Care of the Soul*. New York: HarperPerennial.

Morgenstern, Julie. 1998. *Organizing from the Inside Out*. New York: Owl Books.

Niebuhr, Reinhold. 1943. The Serenity Prayer. In *Bartlett's Familiar Quotations*, sixteenth edition; Justin Kaplan, gen. ed. (Boston: Little, Brown and Co. 1992), 684:14. *God, give us grace to accept with serenity the things that cannot be changed, courage to change the things which should be changed; and the wisdom to distinguish the one from the other.*

Passaris, Silvia John. 1986–1989. Guided Imagery. Workshops and weekly practice. Glendale, Calif.: Healing Light Center Church.

Peale, Norman Vincent. 1992. *The Power of Positive Thinking*. New York: Ballantine's Fawcett Crest. First published by Prentice-Hall, Inc. 1952.

Putnam, Linda. 1983–1984. Assignment of addiction and body papers. Acting class assignment. Northampton, MA: Actor's Space.

Rafkin, Louise. 1998. *Other People's Dirt*. Chapel Hill, N.C.: Algonquin Books of Chapel Hill.

Rowling, J. K. 2000. *Harry Potter and the Goblet of Fire*. New York: Scholastic Press.

———. 1999. *Harry Potter and the Prisoner of Azkaban*. New York: Scholastic Press.

———. 1998. *Harry Potter and the Chamber of Secrets*. New York: Scholastic Press.

———. 1997. *Harry Potter and the Sorcerer's Stone*. New York: Scholastic Press.

Rhys, Jean. 1966. *The Wide Sargasso Sea*. New York: W. W. Norton and Co.

Schepper, Luc de. 1991. *Full of Life*. Los Angeles: Tale Weaver Publishing.

Sendak, Maurice. 1970. *In the Night Kitchen*. New York: Harpercrest.

Silverblatt, Michael. 1999. Bookworm. National Public Radio. Santa Monica, Calif.: KCRW, July.

Simpson, Carol. 1987. Intuitive Awareness Workshop. Glendale, Calif.: Healing Light Center Church.

Smiley, Jane. 1995. The Bathroom. *Home: American Writers Remember Rooms of Their Own,* edited by Sharon Sloan Fiffer and Steve Fiffer. New York: Vintage Books (Random House).

Starhawk. 1987. *Truth or Dare.* New York: Harper & Row.

Teasdale, Sallie. 1995. The Basement. *Home: American Writers Remember Rooms of Their Own,* edited by Sharon Sloan Fiffer and Steve Fiffer. New York: Vintage Books (Random House).

Terkel, Studs. 1996. Interview by Garrison Keillor. Special Broadcast. National Public Radio. Santa Monica: KCRW, August 30. First broadcast November 1995.

Thompson, Richard Frederick. 1985. *The Brain: An Introduction to Neuroscience.* New York: W. H. Freeman and Company.

Ueland, Brenda. 1987. *If You Want to Write: A Book about Art, Independence and Spirit.* Saint Paul, Minn.: Gray Wolf Press. First published by G. P. Putnam, 1938.

Viereck, JohnAlexis. 1988. Healing the light: the integration of the shadow in the new age. Unpublished paper.

Weaver, Lois. 1984–1986. Walk: an improvisational method to develop character for actors. Personal communications. New York: WOW Café.

Whyte, Lancelot Law. 1948. *The Next Development of Man.* New York: The Free Press. Quoted in Jamake Highwater, *The Primal Mind: Vision and Reality in Indian America* (New York: Harper & Row, 1981), xii.

Yee, Mary, ed. 1994. *Do It!: Efficient Housecleaning.* San Francisco: Chronicle Books.

Zanetti, Eugenio (designer for the 1999 movie *The Haunting*). 1999. Style; master of the house. Interview by Amy M. Spindler. *New York Times Sunday Magazine,* July 11.

———. 1989. *The Seat of the Soul.* New York: Fireside Books.

Zukav Gary. 1979. *The Dancing Wu Li Masters.* New York: Bantam Books.

Zweig, Connie, and Steve Wolf. 1997. *Romancing the Shadow: Illuminating the Dark Side of the Soul.* New York: Ballantine Books.

For ten years **Kathryn L. Robyn** helped support herself by cleaning houses while studying healing and transformational theatre. In *Spiritual Housecleaning* she combines her expertise in these two vocations to help others view cleaning as a potential spiritual practice and an opportunity for personal growth. Ms. Robyn is a lifelong activist, artist, and consultant for women's issues and the healing process. She has been participating in and leading transformational workshops and support groups for both women and men recovering from childhood and adult trauma and substance abuse for over twenty years with organizations such as Child Help USA and the Alcoholism Center for Women. Ms. Robyn is a natural energy healer, trained in advanced energy healing, anatomy, body symbology, and meditation. Whether working in tandem with physicians, therapists, or alternative medicine practitioners, or on her own, Ms. Robyn has guided hundreds of people through the healing process, leaving them stronger and more connected with themselves.

Some Other New Harbinger Self-Help Titles

Juicy Tomatoes, $13.95
Help for Hairpullers, $13.95
The Anxiety & Phobia Workbook, Third Edition, $19.95
Thinking Pregnant, $13.95
Rosacea, $13.95
Shy Bladder Syndrome, $13.95
The Adoption Reunion Survival Guide, $13.95
The Queer Parent's Primer, $14.95
Children of the Self-Absorbed, $14.95
Beyond Anxiety & Phobia, $19.95
The Money Mystique, $13.95
Toxic Coworkers, $13.95
The Conscious Bride, $12.95
The Family Recovery Guide, $15.95
The Assertiveness Workbook, $14.95
Write Your Own Prescription for Stress, $13.95
The Shyness and Social Anxiety Workbook, $15.95
The Anger Control Workbook, $17.95
Family Guide to Emotional Wellness, $24.95
Undefended Love, $13.95
The Great Big Book of Hope, $15.95
Don't Leave it to Chance, $13.95
Emotional Claustrophobia, $12.95
The Relaxation & Stress Reduction Workbook, Fifth Edition, $19.95
The Loneliness Workbook, $14.95
Thriving with Your Autoimmune Disorder, $16.95
Illness and the Art of Creative Self-Expression, $13.95
The Interstitial Cystitis Survival Guide, $14.95
Outbreak Alert, $15.95
Don't Let Your Mind Stunt Your Growth, $10.95
Energy Tapping, $14.95
Under Her Wing, $13.95
Self-Esteem, Third Edition, $15.95
Women's Sexualitites, $15.95
Knee Pain, $14.95
Helping Your Anxious Child, $12.95
Breaking the Bonds of Irritable Bowel Syndrome, $14.95
Multiple Chemical Sensitivity: A Survival Guide, $16.95
Dancing Naked, $14.95
Why Are We Still Fighting, $15.95
From Sabotage to Success, $14.95
Parkinson's Disease and the Art of Moving, $15.95
A Survivor's Guide to Breast Cancer, $13.95
Men, Women, and Prostate Cancer, $15.95
Make Every Session Count: Getting the Most Out of Your Brief Therapy, $10.95
Virtual Addiction, $12.95
After the Breakup, $13.95
Why Can't I Be the Parent I Want to Be?, $12.95
The Secret Message of Shame, $13.95
The OCD Workbook, $18.95
Tapping Your Inner Strength, $13.95
Binge No More, $14.95
When to Forgive, $12.95
Practical Dreaming, $12.95
Healthy Baby, Toxic World, $15.95
Making Hope Happen, $14.95
I'll Take Care of You, $12.95
Survivor Guilt, $14.95
Children Changed by Trauma, $13.95
Understanding Your Child's Sexual Behavior, $12.95
The Self-Esteem Companion, $10.95
The Gay and Lesbian Self-Esteem Book, $13.95
Making the Big Move, $13.95
How to Survive and Thrive in an Empty Nest, $13.95
Living Well with a Hidden Disability, $15.95
Overcoming Repetitive Motion Injuries the Rossiter Way, $15.95
What to Tell the Kids About Your Divorce, $13.95
The Divorce Book, Second Edition, $15.95
Claiming Your Creative Self: True Stories from the Everyday Lives of Women, $15.95

Call **toll free, 1-800-748-6273,** or log on to our online bookstore at **www.newharbinger.com** to order. Have your Visa or Mastercard number ready. Or send a check for the titles you want to New Harbinger Publications, Inc., 5674 Shattuck Ave., Oakland, CA 94609. Include $4.50 for the first book and 75¢ for each additional book, to cover shipping and handling. (California residents please include appropriate sales tax.) Allow two to five weeks for delivery.

Prices subject to change without notice.